MEDITATIONS FOR MEN WHO DO NEXT TO NOTHING
(AND WOULD LIKE TO DO EVEN LESS)

ATTENTION: SCHOOLS AND CORPORATIONS

WARNER books are available at quantity discounts with bulk purchase for educational, business, or sales promotional use. For information, please write to: SPECIAL SALES DEPARTMENT, WARNER BOOKS, 1271 AVENUE OF THE AMERICAS, NEW YORK, N.Y. 10020.

ARE THERE WARNER BOOKS
YOU WANT BUT CANNOT FIND IN YOUR LOCAL STORES?

You can get any WARNER BOOKS title in print. Simply send title and retail price, plus 95¢ per order and 95¢ per copy to cover mailing and handling costs for each book desired. New York State and California residents add applicable sales tax. Enclose check or money order only, no cash please, to: WARNER BOOKS, P.O. BOX 690, NEW YORK, N.Y. 10019.

MEDITATIONS FOR MEN WHO DO NEXT TO NOTHING
(AND WOULD LIKE TO DO EVEN LESS)

LEE WARD SHORE

WARNER BOOKS

A Time Warner Company

Warner Books, Inc., 1271 Avenue of the Americas, New York, NY 10020

 A Time Warner Company

Printed in the United States of America
First Printing: June 1994
10 9 8 7 6 5 4 3 2 1

Library of Congress Cataloging-in-Publication Data
Shore, Lee Ward.
   Meditations for men who do next to nothing : and would like to do even less / Lee Ward Shore.
      p.   cm.
   ISBN 0-446-39525-0
   1. Men—Conduct of life—Humor.   I. Title.
PN6231.M45S5   1994
818′.5402—dc20   93-48955
                                                                          CIP

Cover design by Diane Luger

Cover illustration by Carter Goodrich

Book design by L. McRee

To Nicky and Shiva,
the masters of creative inertia

ACKNOWLEDGMENTS

Thanks to all who made this book possible:
Mary Yost, Joann Davis, Grace Sullivan, Sona Vogel,
and Tom Pennacchini.

INTRODUCTION

Choices. Decisions. Responsibilities. As modern men in today's complex world, we face the stress of having to make a vast number of decisions every day, decisions that can have far-reaching, serious effects on our health and happiness, and how often we score with the babes—or, indeed, if we ever do. The sheer volume of choices to make and duties to perform can overwhelm us, especially when we're preoccupied with the hooters on the new gal in Purchasing.

On top of our responsibilities to job, home, and relationships, we can't neglect ourselves. We are challenged to set personal boundaries, to take inventory of ourselves and review old patterns, to let go of the clutter left over from dysfunctional childhoods in our families of origin, to work through the pain, fear, and anger that cause us to be reactors rather than actors. Faced with difficult decisions, like picking point spreads for this weekend's game, we may become paralyzed, dwelling on negative inner dialogues and distorted beliefs that have kept us from connecting in a nurturing, loving way to our inner child and the outer world. Which is a long way of saying our self-absorption is totally justified. Personally, I like to think of myself as a victim of a cold and mechanical society, which is just the kind of deep, introspective thought that impresses chicks at 12 Step meetings (if you haven't discovered them yet, they're a great place for hitting on babes).

Speaking of women, I get exhausted watching the women in my life scurry around like mice, trying to juggle it all. They call themselves Women Who Do Too Much. And they call me a lazy SOB.

Sadly, these gals haven't learned the value of time-out, as we Men Who Do Next to Nothing have. Activity-addicted women try to make us feel guilty for not doing the dishes, participating in child rearing, or stirring from our prone position in front of the tube until the smell of supper hits our nostrils. They demand action. We demand our MTV.

Face it, making choices and decisions is like hitting a pothole on the running track of life. How we handle these unplanned pockmarks in the course will determine the outcome of the race. Do we stumble in the hole? Do we avoid the obstacle in a looping, circuitous detour that costs us valuable time? Do we courageously leap over the hole and risk injury? Or do we stop midcourse, take stock of our situation, and realize that races are stupid: that competition and victory are hollow and what we really want to do is sit down, crack a frosty, turn on the tube, and watch some other loser run the race?

Our course becomes clear when we have the courage to face ourselves, when we dare to be truth speakers. Decisions become easier to make. We accept that it is healthier to follow our nature and shirk responsibility whenever possible than to bow down to the demands of modern life. Of course we would rather golf than clean the garage, rather check out the comic book convention than get that report done for work, rather recreate for five days and work for two—it's certainly more fun than the other way around! Without question, we prefer sitting down to standing up and enjoy lying down best of all. We must listen to our inner voices, which are reflective of a Higher Power telling us to stop and smell the barbecue.

What we need is validation on a daily basis. Hence, I decided to write *Meditations for Men Who Do Next to Nothing (And Would Like to Do Even Less),* a book that would inspire us to fight the good fight, to remain true to ourselves and steadfast in the conviction that the elimination of all activity and decision making from our lives will grant us the serenity we seek.

These meditations include affirmations that will replace those negative tapes in our heads that tell us to work harder, faster, more diligently. Each meditation begins with a quotation, follows with a brief discussion of a personal issue for the day, and concludes with a reminder to help us stay the course.

I decided to use only quotations from men, not because women haven't contributed immensely to our cultural dialogue, but because, oddly enough, I couldn't find any quotations from women on the virtue of inactivity. I used a variety of quotations from men of different ages, cultures, eras, and philosophies. This gathering of men's quotations has proved to me that some of the greatest men of history knew a great deal about doing next to nothing.

This book of meditations was written to inspire men, but I hope that women will read it as well, particularly women who project their own patterns of frenzied workaholism onto their mates. I hope female readers will gain a new understanding of the peace that comes through procrastination and introduce a little inertia into their own hectic routines.

If you do not respond to a particular meditation, bag it and switch on the tube. That's probably what I did when I was writing it. After all, life is meant to be lived at a 180-degree angle.

MEDITATIONS FOR MEN WHO DO NEXT TO NOTHING

(AND WOULD LIKE TO DO EVEN LESS)

STRESS/PRESSURE

Consider the lilies of the field, how they grow; they toil not,
neither do they spin. Yet even Solomon in all his splendor
was not arrayed like one of these.

Matthew 6:28–29

We Men Who Do Next to Nothing can find the beginning of a new day a perplexing and difficult time. All around us people are making agendas, setting lunch dates, and writing "to do" lists. The pressure that the workaholics who inhabit our world exert upon us to join them in their frantic struggle—to get it right, to get up off the couch, to switch off the ball game and lose the beer gut, to spend more time with the family—can be overwhelming.

At trying times like these, it is important to remember that we are fashioned in God's image and perfect just as we are.

Just for today, give me the willingness to do nothing at all.

GETTING AHEAD/ GOAL ORIENTATION

Give me a roof over my head and something to drink, I've got all I need.

Slash

It is only the second day of the work week, but already we Men Who Do Next to Nothing are feeling the pressure to improve ourselves, to make today more productive than yesterday.

Getting ahead is an exacting business that demands sacrifices like getting up in the morning, showering, and putting on a suit. Success requires that we put work before everything else in our lives . . . including football. It insists that we compete and compromise and put off our first beer until noon.

It is time to stop and see what happens to us when we live a goal-oriented life. Are we the men we want to be or the wimps our wives wished they'd married?

I wonder if I am the kind of guy I'd want to sit down and have a beer with?

DISHONESTY

Father, I cannot tell a lie . . .

George Washington

Dishonesty is a milepost on the road to self-deception. When we allow ourselves to give in to deception, we alienate ourselves and those close to us.

Think about it. The last time you swore to your girlfriend that you were finally going to clean the leaves out of the gutters, and then you didn't and the rain backed up and collapsed the ceiling over the cedar closet where her winter wardrobe is stored, what was the result? Negativity? Conflict? An erosion of intimacy?

Although we are surrounded by a society where dishonesty runs rampant, we Men Who Do Next to Nothing must dare to be truth speakers. Be honest. Tell your wife you have no intention of cleaning the gutters or anything else . . . ever. We are the only ones who can choose truth over deception.

There is an old saying, "What's done is done," so why make excuses?

RESPONSIBILITIES/OPTIONS

All work and no play makes Jack a dull boy.

James Howell

We are counseled from the time we are children that work must come before play. Before we can watch cartoons or go to the movies, the chores have to be done. All sorts of cruel and inhuman restrictions are imposed in the name of responsibility. If we want that hot-fudge sundae, we must eat every last lima bean.

We Men Who Do Next to Nothing have learned that work, once begun, is never finished and so is better never begun at all. We have learned how to break the intergenerational chain of the work ethic. We can decide to be different. We can have dessert before dinner. We can read the latest *Playboy* before *The Wall Street Journal*. We can let her bring home the bacon. We have choices.

Let go, let God, let somebody else.

DISCOVERY/INFLEXIBILITY

He was a very valiant man who first adventured on eating of oysters.

James I

Crazy thinking involves the belief that things are better when they are in place, in order, and permanently fixed. So much energy is wasted trying to Super Glue life, but what is inflexible can break. When we become rigid, we lose touch with the rushing creek of life.

Be flexible. Let things lie where they fall. Dirty socks don't always have to go in a hamper. Dinner doesn't always have to be eaten at a table. Where is it written that one must always sleep in a bed at night? What's wrong with a desk top at noon? Why must we always work during the week and rest over the weekend? Why not vice versa?

When we stop experimenting, stop looking, stop asking new questions, it is time to die.

Am I dead, or alive at a 180-degree angle?

WIT/WISDOM

Take my wife . . . please!

Henny Youngman

Wit is a weapon against the onslaught of life. There is nothing like a chuckle to perk up our day, particularly when it is at someone else's expense. Humor, like the miniskirt, is one of the few good reasons to get out of bed each morning.

Sometimes, though, we lose the ability to find the fun in life. We cannot see the humor in ourselves or, more important, in others. If our mates complain that we don't make a living, participate in parenting, or share the housework, and we feel that they are personally attacking us, putting us down, calling us heels, we must reassess our negative thinking.

In moments of personal crisis, humor helps us cope, so try making a funny. Everybody loves a cut-up, and doesn't she always say that your sense of humor is one of the reasons she married you?

Today, I will laugh in the face of adversity, my wife, my boss, or anyone or anything that tries to crush my playful inner child.

SPONTANEITY

Many a man's profanity has saved him from a nervous breakdown.

Henry S. Haskins

Have you ever noticed how much of your day is spent doing two things at once? We lead busy lives: we watch TV and eat dinner, we have sex and watch TV, we eat and breathe, we breathe and watch TV. We are so distracted by our many overlapping activities that we forget how to live in the moment. We forget to savor the simple pleasures that life provides us, inhaling, exhaling, bellowing at the tops of our lungs, or excreting extraneous intestinal gas. This is our human inheritance. Is it wrong to revel in it?

We need to fully experience these simple moments, to feel the fullness of our life force. It is in these personal moments of self-expression that we are truly alive.

Today, let me not only go with the flow, but celebrate it.

ANGER

I never work better than when I am inspired by anger.
Martin Luther

Anger is a hotbed of controversy for us Men Who Do Next to Nothing. Although we understand that anger is not only a healthy outlet but a great motivator, our mates take our anger personally and often react with a host of painful emotional blows that interrupt our peaceful enjoyment of life.

Remember the last time your wife asked you to fix the washer on the kitchen sink and you pulled out your four-hundred-and-fifty-dollar faucet-washer repair kit, but all you managed to do was scratch the stainless steel and break your left index finger? And then you started screaming so loud that she grabbed the wrench out of your hand and in twenty seconds flat fixed the washer, but then refused to sleep with you for a week?

What does this teach us? When our rage brims over the lip of our self-control at the petty annoyances of life, should we bottle it up? Should we seal ourselves off emotionally? Should we give up and call in a professional? No! Anger is our friend, and a wife is cheaper than a plumber.

Anger is not the problem. My wife is.

AFFIRMATION/NEGATION

How can they say my life is not a success? Have I not for more than sixty years got enough to eat and escaped being eaten?

Logan Pearsall Smith

We Men Who Do Next to Nothing should give ourselves more credit. Although the world will tell us that our beer glass is perpetually half-empty, we must remind ourselves that it doesn't much matter because there's half a case left in the fridge.

Workaholics who measure their lives in laundry lists of meaningless accomplishments cannot understand the perfect bliss of utter inactivity. Isn't existing, in and of itself, an art? Isn't regressing to a vegetative state, in fact, a perfect union of man and nature? What does your lawn accomplish each day? It looks happy, doesn't it? No one tells turf to get a job. And it costs a lot of money to maintain.

Take a few moments to applaud the wonder of yourself. In fact, take a few hours. Hell, take a long weekend.

Today is realization day for what I have not accomplished. Celebrations may be in order. Gimme a beer.

PRESENTS

A wise lover values not so much the gift of the lover as the love of the giver.

Thomas à Kempis

It was your anniversary. And you forgot. So you didn't come home with a dozen long-stem roses. You didn't say it with diamonds. Does this mean that you are a bad partner? Isn't it enough that you simply came home? Isn't your very presence enough evidence of your devotion? Doesn't she know what a great catch you are?

What we do with our lives is up to us, and the gift of sharing our destiny with our significant other is the finest present we men can offer. Recite these truths to yourself when she demands more than you can give, when she insists on going out to eat at a restaurant that doesn't accept two-for-one coupons or traveling to a place that does not honor AAA discounts. Don't let her attitude wound your generous inner spirit. All of us have resentments to work through. Just be patient. She'll get over it.

Help me to remember that I am God's gift.

FAILURE

*A man's life is interesting primarily when he has failed—I well
know.*

Georges Clemenceau

When I read a passage like the one above, I am inspired. I
just want to read it over and over again, to remind myself of
how I sometimes suppress everything that is unique and special
in myself in order to accomplish a goal. Usually I end up sick
and sorry with effort, not realizing that everything I need is
right here beside me: my cable guide, my remote control, and
my family size bag of Doritos.

This passage is beautiful testimony to the fruits of failure. Do
you think successful guys have time to contemplate what is
truly interesting in life, like which bar to hit tonight, who
should be on the All-Madden team this year, or how to pick up
that hot new babe in Purchasing? Of course not. They're too
busy working.

Help me to remember that still waters run deep.

FELLOWSHIP/AFFECTION

Love and do what you will.

St. Augustine

It is impossible to watch the ball game and be intimate at the same time. It takes energy to be intimate, to express fellowship and affection, to do what is necessary to communicate with our mates. Being together is a lot of work.

Surprisingly, our significant others don't seem to understand this. They demand that we reach out, reach in, reach over, and reach through. Just the words alone are enough to exhaust us.

We must explain to those we love that intimacy with another is not possible unless we have achieved intimacy with ourselves. This requires taking the time to rest, to contemplate, to reorganize our collection of athletic socks, or to put a sixth coat of Turtle Wax on the Mustang. In order to merge spiritually with my spouse, I must first become my own best friend. And so I must ask myself, what would my best friend do for me to express his devotion? Certainly tickets to the next pennant race would be a good start.

Intimacy, like a hangover, begins at the ball park.

PRODUCTIVITY/CREATIVITY

We will sell no wine before its time.

Ernest and Julio Gallo

Many people believe that it is the workaholics in this world who are the most fruitful, the most productive, and the most creative. Not so! We Men Who Do Next to Nothing realized long ago that overextended deadlines and frantic, anxiety-ridden activity never produce anything of quality. True creativity, like most of the finer things in this world, must be allowed to age sufficiently, and we are experts at that.

So the next time your mother asks you what you think you are doing sleeping your life away, or shrieks that you haven't moved for a week and are stinking up the family room, or demands that you strap on your tool belt and complete that kitchen addition you began eighteen months ago, tell her that you are ripening, fermenting, and will get up only when you have reached your peak flavor. Otherwise, your vintage bouquet may be severely compromised. Men, like fine wine, require absolute stillness in dark cool rooms to achieve peak performance.

Rome wasn't built in a day, so why should your kitchen addition be any different?

GRUDGES

The only things one never regrets are one's mistakes.
Oscar Wilde

Nurturing grudges seems to be the favorite pastime of some people. So you forgot to pick up your mother after her doctor's appointment and she had to take three buses through the seediest neighborhood in town. She got home okay, so why dwell on it? What's she gonna do, disinherit you?

And so you forgot to tell your wife about the night crawlers you were storing in the empty dip container until she tried to serve it at her Lamaze class get-together. It's not all that different from sushi, so what's the big deal? Pregnant women are always throwing up anyway. Or perhaps you left the "Dear Fuck-face" salutation in your most recent report to the stockholders. Computer glitches happen all the time.

When faced with the consequences of your actions or inactions you can hold on to the pain, the shame, and the blame, or you can utter the magic words *I'm sorry* and move on. Recognize that grudges serve no purpose, and those who hold them are simply victims of their own inability to chill out. What a shame! Thank goodness we aren't stuck in a victim mentality.

Forgiveness is a gift you give yourself.

CIVILIZED BEHAVIOR

Labor is the curse of the world, and nobody can meddle with it without becoming proportionately brutified.

Nathaniel Hawthorne

Has civilization really progressed? Our prehistoric ancestors risked their lives hunting to provide food for the clan. Today, we risk the L.A. freeways at rush hour. The ancient tribes of Europe, Asia, and Africa slaughtered each other to secure their enemies' land and resources for themselves. Today, we park in loading zones and Handicapped Only spaces to get a jump on anybody else who was thinking of buying a few cases of antifreeze at the Walgreens dollar day sale.

It seems we are still engaged in a ruthless, barbarous struggle to increase our riches and engine temperature at the expense of our fellow beings. Wouldn't it be more civilized to avoid contributing to those bad vibes on the freeway and just sleep in today? And if parking is a problem, send your little sister on her bike to pick up your lottery tickets and Alka-Seltzer. Park yourself on the porch, where you can't do any harm.

If it's here today, it'll be here tomorrow, so what's your hurry?

IDENTITY

I do not know myself, and God forbid that I should.
Johann Wolfgang von Goethe

As men, we have been conditioned to define ourselves in relation to the outside world. We have been conditioned to identify ourselves in terms of what we do rather than what we are. No wonder we feel pressured to do something beyond moving our bowels on a regular basis.

An important part of recovery is finding out who we really are, beyond what others expect of us, beyond what we do, beyond what we earn.

Who is this person I call me? Am I the guy who schlepps to the office every morning to sell the gadgets that mechanically screw the tops onto tubes of toothpaste, or am I a secret agent in a red Alfa-Romeo with a Rolex watch and a beautiful blonde on each arm? Maybe I'm a lead guitarist for a heavy metal band, in a red Alfa-Romeo with a Rolex watch and a beautiful blonde on each arm. I mean, maybe I'm not, but the possibilities are certainly worth considering. Besides, self-discovery is a lot more fun than working.

Today, I will begin an inner journey of self-discovery that, with any luck, will last the rest of my life, or at least until happy hour.

HUMOR

What's a perfect ten?
> *A three-foot-tall girl with no teeth and a flat head so you can put your beer down.*

Ricardo Panadero

I love jokes like the one above. They have such a refreshing way of cutting right through to the meat of things.

How often have we had whimsical, youthful thoughts yet have prevented ourselves from enjoying them because we are in mixed company. We think of a funny but do not share it because we are repressed. People curl their lips at us and hiss that we are politically incorrect. This is of course infinitely preferable to having a martini thrown in our faces, but it still can be embarrassing at a get-together.

What people, especially the people our girlfriends invite to cocktail parties, have forgotten is that to be male is to be politically incorrect. It's a package deal. We come naturally by a mischievous, boyish sense of fun. We should not be shamed into swallowing our punch lines. Which reminds me of the one about the sword swallower and the stallion.

Why can't everybody lighten up?

F—— 'em if they can't take a joke.

LIVING LIFE FULLY

He who draws upon his own resources easily comes to the end of his wealth.

William Hazlitt

We can get so obsessed with possessing things that we often find ourselves being possessed rather than possessing the trappings of a successful life. We can get so caught up in the need to own things—a house; a laser disc player; a thirty-inch, high-resolution television; a self-sharpening combination band saw and electric sander; a portable CD player with a belt attachment—that we end up slaves to our definitions of success.

We need to teach ourselves and our girlfriends that men are like pigeons. All pigeons do is hang around in parks all day, yet have you ever seen a skinny one? No? And why? Because they are free to live off other people's crumbs, other people's possessions, and therefore have no need to acquire their own, with the exception, of course, of the laser disc player, which, pigeons or not, I'm buying first thing next week.

Am I content to fully appreciate what I do not possess? I think so. Although if I get the laser disc player, I guess I'll have to go ahead and get some laser discs. And my speakers are shot. What good is a laser disc player without good speakers? And my receiver really rots. What I really need is a whole new setup.

GOALS

Let's face it, the first tours the Beatles did, the main essential thing was scoring chicks.

Paul McCartney

In trying to reach our goals, we can develop tunnel vision. We visualize the end of our efforts and become obsessed with the finish line or the bottom line. We forget that the real reward comes when we remove all lines from our lives and just concentrate on the bottoms, in every sense of the word.

When we rush, rush, rush, we can forget that true enjoyment comes from the process. We overlook the violets along the path. We forget about the position that guy in the locker room was describing. Where was her left leg supposed to go again?

In a perfect world, there would be no finish lines and all women would be double-jointed.

DECISION MAKING

*When a man hasn't a good reason for doing a thing, he has a
good reason for letting it alone.*

Sir Walter Scott

How often as Men Who Do Next to Nothing do we feel ourselves pressured to hurry up and make a decision, like which brand of garden weasel to buy or what to do with our lives?

Of course the problem is once we make those decisions, we come under pressure to act on them. Once we go ahead and buy our weasel of preference, we may actually have to weed. Once we decide what to do with our lives, the implication is that we go ahead and do it.

Isn't it much easier to avoid making any decisions in the first place? Isn't it healthier to avoid asking leading questions of ourselves or, in fact, asking any questions at all, of anybody, at any time? If we avoid thinking about the issues in our lives, we stay clear of the activity danger zone.

If an issue falls in the forest and I'm not there to hear it, does it exist? Who cares? I hate hiking.

QUIET TIME

Edith, stifle!

Archie Bunker

Every day we are bombarded by renegade channels assaulting our own personal networks. We're distracted by traffic, the neighbors, our girlfriends, the neighbors' girlfriends. And everybody wants to discuss something just when your favorite shows are coming on. Your wife wants to talk about your relationship, your boss wants to discuss the ten grand missing from the Anderson account. Why can't they wait until a more convenient time, like the next Ice Age, for example?

We even have difficulty sleeping because we're constantly interrupted by clients calling during business hours.

We have to tune out the complaints, the ultimatums, and the threats of violence or legal action and tune in to ourselves. After all, we've got the best fall lineup going.

Quiet time lets me star in my own life.

WISDOM/KNOWLEDGE

*Tomorrow a stranger will say with masterly good sense pre-
cisely what we have thought and felt all the time.*
Ralph Waldo Emerson

Oh, how we underestimate our own wisdom. Then that
stranger comes by and reminds us of what we knew all along
but temporarily forgot because, of course, short-term memory
loss is an unavoidable part of living.

Of course we understand those new memo-routing proce-
dures at work. We understand the president's new economic
plan. We knew you're not supposed to put aluminum foil in the
microwave.

Deep down, we know. We know that we know, even though
we forgot. That tax advice our friend gave us, you know, that
bit about mailing your return before April 15? We knew that.
That suggestion Dad gave us about approaching the boss with
a smile and a handshake instead of an automatic weapon? We
knew that. The stuff that professor at Joe's party was saying
about quantum physics and its relationship to time and matter
in a spatial universe? We knew that, too. We just need a little
memory jog now and again.

**Buried deep in my subconscious lie the answers to life's
greatest questions. Anybody got a shovel?**

FAMILY

Get away from me, kid, you bother me.

W. C. Fields

Years ago, Mom and Pop, Grandma and Grandpa, and all the little children gathered together in front of the radio to laugh with Jack Benny or Uncle Milty, to wonder wide-eyed how the Shadow always knew or who that masked man really was.

But now with a television in every room, urban alienation, and the ability to put physical and emotional miles between families and their offspring, the parlor of yesteryear is considerably quieter. Thank God.

But we can still share quality time with the little kiddies. If they want to watch *Three's Company* and then see the Giants take on Phoenix, they can hang out, as long as they keep quiet and bring their own bag of Chee-tos. I mean, that's life, right? They're gonna have to learn eventually that they don't get to call the channels when there is someone bigger than them holding the remote control, and they better come equipped to provide for their own nourishment. These are invaluable lessons of modern life that I am duty bound to impart to my kids.

Football is a metaphor for life.

HOPES AND DREAMS

Hope is independent of the apparatus of logic.

Norman Cousins

As boys, we had high hopes for the future. As men we are told that the future is now, so we better forget about that Stratocaster we've always wanted or those vintage Spiderman comic books and start locking in interest rates on long-term CDs.

Now this really enrages my inner child. I was really getting close to buying that guitar. It's electric purple, with orange flames climbing up the neck. The guy told me Jimi Hendrix once sat on that guitar because somebody had left it lying on a chair, and Jimi just sat on it because he was so distracted because he was right at that moment mentally composing "Purple Haze." See, the song was originally called "Purple Bass," on account of he was sitting on my guitar, but the record company made him change it on the LP.

When you think of it, it's really an investment. A guitar like that is bound to go up more than 2.3 percent compounded monthly.

To hell with the future, I want my guitar.

SELF-AWARENESS

Any desire for self-improvement is petty.

J. Krishnamurti

In the race to get ahead, get better, get successful, we risk the danger of not appreciating fully the things that truly make life worth living, like lunch or dinner. In fact, working, rushing around, leaves us little time to be fully conscious of what our bodies are telling us, which is usually one of three things: I'm hungry, I'm thirsty, or I'm in the mood.

The work world would have us think of our bodies as nonexistent, but what could be more important? Who would work when he could drink instead, or eat, or excrete? Doesn't the ultimate appreciation of life reside in our bodies? Isn't it a crime against nature to turn a deaf ear to the most basic demands of our physical selves?

I better take the time to listen and respond to my body's demands. It's the only fun I'm going to get out of life.

CURIOSITY/TAKING IT TO THE LIMIT

Curiosity is one of the permanent and certain characteristics of a vigorous intellect.

Samuel Johnson

As I look back on my greatest adventures in life, I realize that most of them would never have happened had I stuck to the straight and narrow. Like the time I wandered into the Sail and Rail down by the freight yard, a real man's kind of bar where your elbows stick to the tables and the smell of fine draft blends congenially with industrial disinfectant. And they don't serve frozen daiquiris.

I sat down next to an old salt who sucked down Wild Turkey like he was born with bourbon for blood, and after about the eighth round, he got kind of talkative. He told me about his stint as the owner of a Shanghai bordello, a profitable establishment very similar in style to the Sail and Rail, which had been financed for him by some guy named Vic the Throat. He never told me how Vic had earned his name. I was only on my fourth bourbon, and perhaps he deemed me unworthy. And I never did get the moral of the story, but he taught me a great card trick, which I use all the time at poker parties.

Life is full of wonderful mysteries for those willing to check out the side streets. Just be sure to set your car alarm.

BEING IN CHARGE

It is a fine thing to command, even if it be only a herd of cattle.
Miguel de Cervantes

As born leaders, we think that we must do it all. How self-centered of us to think we are the only ones who can get it done and get it done right!

Of course, I'm not talking about highly complex tasks calling for an expertise that only we can bring to bear on a particular project, like grilling burgers. I'm talking about jobs that we could delegate. Like hot dogs; it's impossible to screw those up. I mean, they're precooked.

The thing with hot dogs is if you cut them in half, then you've got it knocked. It's pretty much a matter of even heat distribution, and that's it. Burgers, on the other hand, have to be finessed, or they go dry on the outside and raw on the inside. Also, you have to be pretty handy with a spatula to turn those quarter pounders without leaving an eighth of a pound still stuck to the grill.

So the idea is, leave yourself free to focus all your attention on the tough stuff, like burgers, and be man enough to let your wife turn the dogs.

Besides, if she screws it up, she's gonna eat them anyway. I'm certainly not going to. Do you have any idea what they put in those things?

INTEGRITY

[T]his above all: to thine own self be true . . .
William Shakespeare

I wonder. Have I sacrificed my integrity in the race to get ahead? Am I opting for peace in the home over peace of mind? Am I listening to my mate when I should be listening to myself? Am I going to give in and paint the ceiling, or stand firm and go golfing like I planned?

Every day presents another opportunity to betray myself. Do I get up when my alarm rings or stay in bed until I'm not tired anymore? Do I get on the train to work, even though I'd rather stick needles in my eyes than commute one more day? Do I buy Billy braces or that rookie Ernie Banks card? Do I wear the new starched oxford or the soft flannel, with the precisely engineered ventilation system in the elbows, that I've spent fifteen years weathering to perfection? Do I live my life sitting up, when I'd much rather be lying down?

It is easy to forget to listen to myself. I gobble up these bits of integrity slippage like potato chips, and no one can eat just one. How important it is to stop and look at what I'm doing. What a relief to realize that underneath the pile of orthodontist bills, I can still find my self-respect ready to reconnect with me just as soon as I am willing to sit down and take a load off.

So what if my life resembles a garbage dump? I like it that way.

FEELING OVERWHELMED/ DISAPPEARING

In managing human affairs, there is no better rule than self-restraint.

Lao-tse

From the moment we wake up till we drift off to sleep hours or minutes later, we are bombarded with information to be processed. We begin to feel machinelike, computing it all: Which side of the street can I park on this morning? Is this recycling day, or tomorrow? Is today clean underwear day, or is it next Tuesday?

Then we reach for the morning paper, and there is nothing but more bad news. John Elway still hasn't won a Super Bowl. Another supermodel is dating a rock star instead of us. Rain is predicted for Saturday and Sunday. It's a bleak forecast all the way around; no wonder we feel overwhelmed.

As Men Who Do Next to Nothing, we are only just taking baby steps toward learning the process of prioritizing, allowing ourselves to block out the trivia, to exercise self-restraint in our encounters with reality. Is it really important to know the name of our senator or if there is right on red in this state? I don't think so.

When we clean our mental houses, we find serenity, along with a half-dozen dust bunnies and last month's Visa bill.

REALITY/FANTASY

Ever let the fancy roam,
Pleasure never is at home.

John Keats

People who are "experts" on the subject tell us that one of the danger signals of poor mental health is losing the ability to distinguish between reality and fantasy. A sick man, they tell us, builds a fantasy and then moves right in.

We Men Who Do Next to Nothing must learn to ask ourselves and our mates, "Yeah, and so what?" What is wrong with living a fantasy? Who would rather live real life as a systems analyst when he could live a fantasy life as Eddie Vedder? Who needs to sweat real blood to make the mortgage payments on a prefab suburban dump when he could live in a fantasy palace of his own design, rent free? What is the big deal about reality, anyway?

It's not that we don't perceive reality, we just choose not to live in it.

SILENCE/INNER PEACE

Silence is deep as Eternity; speech is shallow as Time.
Thomas Carlyle

When we still our minds, we may find inner peace that renews and strengthens us. Or, if you're like me, you'll catch a few much needed, well-deserved winks, which is certainly far more valuable than some abstract spirituality thing.

Frankly, few things stimulate my spirituality more than my wife talking to me. Somehow she inspires me to clear my mind of thoughts, still my brain waves, and cease all mental activity. I enjoy this inner peace, and I am calm as I bond with my Higher Power within, at least until she severs my cosmic line of communication and demands that I actually answer her.

Silence is the sound of our Higher Power calling us. Noise is usually my wife.

RESPONSIBILITY

Is life worth living?

Samuel Butler

As men, we have been raised to take care of our families. Yet down deep, we often have a secret wish that someone else would take care of us. Frequently, we wish we could be stowaways instead of ticketed passengers on the garbage scow of life. Who wants to pay for a ticket on a trash barge, anyway? Come to think of it, they should pay us to ride. We ought to get a salary just for agreeing to exist.

Unfortunately, life is a nonprofit organization supported solely by volunteers, but as volunteers we do have options. For one thing, we can exercise some choice over our destination. We can demand that the scow go someplace besides, say, New Jersey. For another thing, we have the right to pick and choose the tasks we undertake. For instance, we can decline to scrub between our toes or, in fact, to scrub anything at all. We don't have to separate glass and cans, and they can't make us provide for our families or contribute to a more humane global economy. We're volunteers, so what are they gonna do . . . fire us? Dock our pay?

To participate in our lives does not mean that we have to go to New Jersey.

ANGER

@#!! +@**%#@!!*

Axl Rose

Anger is a powerful force. When we become truly enraged we may feel overwhelmed by the force of our feeling and attempt to bottle up our emotions. Inevitably, though, our anger builds to the boiling point, and we explode, often with disastrous results. We get fired. We get thrown out of bars. We get blood on the carpet.

How much better it is to express anger at the moment we begin to experience it. There are so many opportunities to let off steam and avoid nuclear meltdown, if only we would avail ourselves of them.

Say your secretary misspells a client's name or misplaces a preposition. Say your wife serves your dinner and the broccoli's cold. Let them have it. You'll all be better off in the long run if you get those feelings out. And the best part is that next time your broccoli will be hot.

It is the angry young man who gets the multimillion-dollar recording contract and the groupies.

TRANQUILLITY

Periods of tranquillity are seldom prolific of creative achievement.

Alfred North Whitehead

Sometimes people confuse peace and tranquillity with catatonia. In fact, although many of the outward symptoms are similar, they are very different states of being.

Tranquillity comes after watching eight solid hours of NBA playoff action, during which you move nothing more than two eyeballs, a right index finger, and occasionally a vocal cord or two. Peace comes when we still our minds and our bodies, when our jaw hangs slack, when our boxers bag down along with our hopes for the future. Peace comes when we relax, let go of the guilt and most of the sensory awareness of our surrounding environment.

Come to think of it, we might be giving catatonia a bum rap.

FOCUS/CONCENTRATION/ PRIORITIES

My hobbies are hooking up stuff to see if it works, and beer.
                                                        Joe Walsh

Have you ever watched Minnesota Fats play pool? He has total focus. He knows he has to block out everything around him so he can sink that next shot. He knows what his priorities are.

When we try to focus like this in our own lives, people around us tell us we are rude and inattentive. They don't appreciate the intense concentration it requires to work out the Sunday *Times* puzzle, tie a fly, or eat a chili burrito properly, savoring every bit and feeling it work its way through our lower intestine.

Of course we didn't notice we knocked over the ashtray, and now the cat is chewing on last night's cigarette butts and tracking ashes all over the new carpet. Actually, we hadn't noticed that burn mark in the middle of it, either. Or the mud we must've tracked in—it is mud, isn't it?

The point is, we've got to focus to get important tasks done. These magical moments when we give our complete and undivided attention to a task put us in touch with our Higher Power. We can get in touch with the carpet cleaner tomorrow.

Focusing allows me to be at one with myself and my own little world. I think I'll stay there for a while. I think the rent's cheaper.

EXPLORATION

. . . to boldly go where no man has gone before.
Mission of the USS *Enterprise*

Not just to go, but to go boldly. I think that means never asking for directions. It means that when faced with new adventures in life or major decisions, such as whether to go left or to go right, we must boldly go left, without relying on maps or lame instructions from gas station workers who can't even navigate gas through a hose.

We must not be afraid of the unexpected intersections of life, even if we've passed one three times in the last half hour. This could be a new shortcut. In a sense, we know where we are going. I mean, knowledge is relative, as are the directions to Aunt Sally's. Funny, but I don't remember passing that burned-out building last time or circling the airport parking lot three times, but memory, too, is relative.

Life is what happens while you're circling the airport.

SELFLESSNESS

He who undervalues himself is justly undervalued by others.
William Hazlitt

The arrogance of our disease fools us into thinking that self-lessness means denying our own egos. But if we give up our egos, what is left?

How can we offer anything to anybody if we abandon ourselves? And think of what a loss to the world it would be if we could no longer offer it our unique and special gifts.

Who would keep our wives in line, curb their spending, instruct them in how to stack the refrigerator so that nothing ever drips on our beer cans? Who would tell our secretaries that "occasional" has two *c*'s and one *s*? Who would tell our kids that a liberal arts education is a waste of time? Without us, they'll be studying useless stuff like Shakespeare or something they call "communication," which, it seems to me, no college in the world can teach you.

Obviously, without our intervention the world would run amok. I'm going to speak up more often.

I have a lot to offer others, and I'm going to make sure they know about it.

THOUGHTS/OPINIONS

To lie still and think little is medicine for the soul.
Friedrich Nietzsche

How many times have we heard it said that we men are creatures of the mind, that we are logical, linear, rational, and left-brained? Could this be true? Are we truly better thinkers than women? It is certainly nice to think so.

Maybe, as heirs to this intellectual tradition of men, we should put our minds to use. Maybe we should work toward envisioning and creating a better world. Maybe we should fulfill our potential as intellectual adventurers, cognitive conquerors, mental world movers. But then again . . . maybe not.

Today, I will not clutter my mind with thoughts.

INTEGRATION/SELFHOOD

To love oneself is the beginning of a life-long romance.
Oscar Wilde

People tell me I'm selfish because I put my needs before the needs of others. She doesn't like it when I opt to watch the bout on Tuesday night instead of going to Aunt Marilyn's funeral. She gets incensed because I like to save old boxes in case I have to move in a hurry one day. She grows irate because I saw no harm in borrowing the shower curtain to use as a tarp on a camping weekend. Hey, water's water, right? She disapproves because I figure if you can't see it, it's not there, so why clean it or pay for it? Who cares what's behind the refrigerator? When am I going to use medical insurance?

As a result of this impervious and all-inclusive disapproval, we Men Who Do Next to Nothing can sometimes get the idea that we are unappreciated. Guilt can rain on our parade of confidence and self-esteem. But men are more than the sum of their character flaws, and the world would be a pretty dull place if there were no secrets behind the refrigerator. We are like rainbows, adding contrast and excitement to a world of women workaholics who have never had the guts or the imagination to sleep under the stars on a shower curtain.

Today, I own up to myself. I own myself, and I could own a lot more if Aunt Marilyn had left me something in the will.

GROWTH

[T]he crooked roads without improvement are roads of genius.
William Blake

Somehow, we all harbor the secret hope that if we can just get ourselves together, if we can finally work out all our issues, plumb the depths of our strengths and weaknesses, and get a grip, then at last, life will leave us alone to catch a few solid z's before the bout starts.

What a shock it is to realize that, like my wife, life never lets up, never leaves me alone, no matter how much money I make, no matter if I clean the garage five times a weekend and finish every household project I've begun in the last ten years—it never, ever, has the common human decency to leave me alone for just five minutes. Just when I think I'm free and clear, and I've settled back onto the couch, it's something else again, like the lawn, or the plugged-up chimney, or the unpaid electric bill, or a new sin tax. It's always something.

How much easier it would be to just avoid growth altogether, to toss away our emotional twin blade and remain spiritually unshaven.

To grow and to change is the normal state for human beings. I am a human being. Maybe there's something I can do to change that.

HINDRANCE/COMPLETION

God keep me from ever completing anything.

Herman Melville

We are often told that there is a purpose behind life's tribulations. There are people who would have us believe that we grow from the challenges that confront us and that every obstacle we hurdle increases our character. These people are women.

We Men Who Do Next to Nothing know that there is no use slugging it out with what is obviously preordained anyway. These things are prearranged by our Higher Power. Who are we to question what is obviously in the cards?

Women don't understand this kind of reasoning. They think that if we don't get a promotion, swing the vacation time, or finance the mortgage, it's our fault. "You got yourself into this, now you can get yourself out" is a common catchphrase, as if we had something to do with what is going on around us. As if it is really within our power to confront the forces at work in our lives.

It is best at times like these to tread a line of least resistance. True, life isn't fair, but neither are women, so nod your head, grunt occasionally, but if she insists on action, let her do it.

An obstacle isn't an obstacle until you try to overcome it.

COURAGE

Of all the thirty-six alternatives, running away is best.
Chinese proverb

How true. And what a perfect formula for a happy life, if only we can find the spiritual serenity to put down our pens, our fists, our memos, and our cellular phones and run like hell to the nearest corner bar.

What has ever been accomplished through competition? Ulcers, high blood pressure, rampant anxiety, urban blight. Are these the legacies we wish to leave to the future? Would we rather say to our grandchildren, "Yes, I stayed, I fought, I worked my whole life in order to retire and live on a fixed income that won't even let me buy the brand of toilet paper with the baby oil on it"? Or would we rather say, "No, I refused, I laid down on the couch, I turned on the television, and now I live on the same fixed income, but I don't need the brand of toilet paper with the baby oil on it because I avoided the stress and don't have to contend with irritated-bowel syndrome"?

Brave men take naps where workaholics fear to tread.

BEAUTY

The most beautiful subjects? The simplest, and the least clad.
                                              Anatole France

How long has it been since we have allowed ourselves to rejoice in a beautiful woman? How long has it been since we have allowed ourselves to tip back our head, to break the crisp morning air with a heartfelt wolf whistle, to follow our fancy, trotting just beside that gorgeous, big-haired brunette headed in the opposite direction of our office? Be honest with yourself. How long has it really been? Two, maybe three days? This is a good indication that your priorities are out of order.

When we live and work in cities, or even when we don't, there are endless opportunities to appreciate the gifts Mother Nature has bestowed upon us. There are tall gifts and short gifts, blonde gifts and redheaded gifts. There are gifts that are built like brick shit houses. We must remember where our priorities truly lie. We must learn to look away from that computer screen and take in the miracles around us.

If we want to appreciate beauty more, we are going to have to work less.

I long for the awareness to say, "Oh, what a glorious piece of ass."

FINANCIAL SECURITY

I spend money on, what—snakes, guitars, and cars.

Slash

It's okay to have money. It's best to have a lot of it if possible. In fact, no matter how much we have, it's never enough. Money, of course, is simply an abstract concept, but it can change into anything we desire: Porsches, imported Scotch, or state-of-the-art electronic equipment. Most important, though, money can buy leisure. Money means you can pay somebody else to shovel your walk, fix your car, paint your apartment, raise your kids, or even occupy your wife for an afternoon if there's a good football game on. Just tell her to go shopping. Women love that.

Of course, earning money is another matter. Actually working for the stuff can turn into a dangerous and frantic need to labor, accumulate, and hoard. A man may deny himself and his conscience in a lifelong, heedless pursuit of hollow capital gain, so it you can, arrange to inherit a fortune or, if you cannot, marry one.

Financial security is okay as long as I don't have to work for it.

SERIOUSNESS/ RESPONSIBILITY/PRIORITIES

I never go jogging, it makes me spill my martini.

George Burns

Straighten that tie. Haul that ass. Get that job, because it's been six years since you earned a decent living. How many of these tapes play over and over again in our minds?

When we hear the negative inner voices or, more often, the negative outer ones nagging at us to get our act together, to grow up, to get serious, we can become tempted to chuck our carefully cultivated patterns of avoidance and become just like everybody else, productive and miserable.

Stop! Stop it right now! Smell those roses. Breathe in that fresh country air. Breathe in carbon monoxide fumes if you have to. Anything's better than becoming an activity addict.

There are only twenty-four hours in each day, and you've already spent half of them asleep. Do you want to spend the other half in a mind-deadening occupation? If you died tomorrow, would you regret that promotion you didn't get because you called in sick forty-seven times in six months, or would you regret that you never hit the road on that Harley you've always dreamed of, with that leggy blonde out of your wildest bondage fantasies clinging to your leather fringe?

Which would you rather have for lunch, a hot dog or a hot hog? Set your priorities and stick to them. It's later than you think.

RISK TAKING

*I'm a Sagittarian ... half man, half horse, with a license to shit
in the streets.*

Keith Richards

Safety, boredom, monogamy. Sometimes I think they're all one and the same. Crazy thinking tells us that if we take risks, we will get caught, but that's our disease talking.

We can take risks. We can flirt with disaster, with danger, with the babe in Purchasing. We can ride that untamed mechanical stallion at Cow Chip Charlie's. We don't fear reprisal. The phone is broken at Cow Chip's, so how can she expect us to call home?

If we weren't meant to drive any faster than 55 MPH, then how come they make Mustangs that can hit 85 in 40.4 seconds on a straightaway? Besides, the cops are mostly in Chevys, so they can't catch you, and if they can't catch you, how are they going to give you a ticket?

We can dance with the devil. We can dance with Linda and Evelyn and Suzanne. We can live like outlaws, at least until last call at Cow Chip's.

I have courage, I have conviction, I have a damn good lawyer.

IN TOUCH/AWARENESS/ LIVING IN THE MOMENT

Hey, Rog, what's happening?

Rerun

What's happening indeed? What's the scoop, the skivvy, the lowdown? Who's in, who's out, who has been benched for the season for having pine tar on his glove? When is Elway going to win a Super Bowl? Is Bud Dry really drier? How many Bon Jovi fans really did keep the faith?

Caught up in our dis-ease, we forget that there's a world going on out there while we're at work. Each day for eight hours plus, we're out of the loop. We don't know what's happening. We don't know who was on Arsenio last night. What's with Darryl Hannah and John-John? When did they take all the music videos off MTV? When did they start putting headlights on sneakers?

Let's face it, the world is a rapidly changing and complicated mosaic of events and personalities. It's a full-time job just keeping up with current events. Who has time to earn a living?

I'd rather be in the swing than in a sling.

REPENTANCE/WISDOM

To repent nothing is the beginning of wisdom.

Ludwig Börne

Wouldn't it be boring if our lives were completely predictable? How tiresome to resolve each and every crisis right when it happens. Life's little surprises can be enlivening affirmations of existence.

Yet how easy it is to become resentful when old skeletons we have long ago shut in a closet and forgotten about suddenly resurface, rattling ancient bones. How unpleasant it can become when events that happened at a panty raid on a sorority house after twelve tequilas when we were twenty-seven suddenly resurface when we are forty, signaling us that they need to be worked through or, at the very least, compensated monetarily.

At moments of crisis like this I ask myself, Can I really believe my inner processes were responsible? I mean, after all, how could she have recognized me with a pair of panties over my head?

There is something within me that knows more than I do. Hopefully, it won't tell anyone else.

CONTROL/ATTITUDE

To be crazy is not necessarily to writhe in snake pits or converse with imaginary gods. It can sometimes be not knowing what to do in the morning.

Christopher Lehman-Haupt

Slowly but surely we are recovering. We are learning to live one day at a time, to not expect too much of ourselves, to take life easy, to smell the dandelions. But sometimes, come nine-fifteen on a traffic-choked freeway, those old panic patterns set in.

I should've gotten up by 8:30 like I planned. It takes longer than twelve minutes to go twelve miles at rush hour. I should've finished writing that presentation I have to give this morning. Do I have the papers I need for the meeting? Did I leave them in that hotel room? What was her name again? She was over eighteen, wasn't she? Why won't this traffic move, for God's sake?

It's probably a bus. It's always a bus. There should be mandatory sentences for drivers who wreck their buses. They should get the chair for causing this kind of mayhem when people are trying to get to work on time. But they don't, they get a coffee break. The guy's probably standing there, having his coffee and doughnut. He doesn't have to get to work. He's at work. He's getting paid to stand there with his coffee and his Boston cream. He's laughing at me. He's dunking his doughnut and laughing at me.

If I cannot control the world, how can they expect me to get to work on time?

EXPECTATIONS/FAILURES

There is much to be said for failure. It is more interesting than success.

Max Beerbohm

When we experience failure, this is usually a good indication that our goals were too high. Lower your expectations, preferably beneath what you know to be your level of achievement, and success is virtually guaranteed.

The fact is the world is a cutthroat, coldhearted place where nice guys usually finish last, so why plan on finishing at all? Why not run half the race, quit before you're winded, and join the babes in the stands watching the other schmucks limp through the finish line? When the race is over, all those babes are gonna be looking for some attention, attention that the guys who finished the race aren't going to be able to give them because they're too tuckered out from all that senseless race running.

Okay, so the egghead back in school who always ruined the grade curve, that jerk in Finance who always works until eight o'clock at night, and the brownnoser who sucks up to the boss instead of throwing bar dice with us real men is gonna run a better race come eight A.M. But what are they going to get for their efforts, ultimately? Bad knees and fallen arches.

I'd rather do without the gain. I have a low threshold for pain, and I'm kind of fond of my arches.

DESPAIR/HOPELESSNESS

Show me a good loser and I'll show you a loser.
Jimmy Carter

Do you remember the day you hit bottom? It was raining, so you pulled out your umbrella, the cabana-size one with the fancy logo that you went to such pains to pinch from the VP of Finance at last year's Christmas party. And guess what? It leaked. All that trouble for a leaky umbrella.

That was the moment you realized that all your hard work and sacrifice would ultimately get you nowhere. The depths of despair were so low that you realized there was nowhere to go but up, and since you knew you weren't going there, you suddenly realized that there was nowhere to go at all.

That's when the sun came out. The clouds lifted, and the sky grew bright and blue. You pulled out the lawn chair of life, the suntan lotion of hope, cranked up the boom box of self-esteem, and basked in the sunshine of self-love. Having nowhere else to go, you began to live in the process. You accepted your powerlessness and forgave yourself for working all those years. You let despair dissipate into the stratosphere and bagged some serious rays.

If the way to the top is uphill, I'll set up camp down here at the bottom.

UNIQUENESS/FEELING SPECIAL

If there is such a thing as genius—which is what . . . what the fuck is it?—I am one, and if there isn't, I don't care.

John Lennon

Am I normal? Am I crazy? Am I an overlooked genius who by some stroke of terrible luck got stuck with this job, this apartment, this hairline? What hidden wonders lie beneath my hair plugs?

Perhaps in a former life I was a great warrior, a dragon slayer, a pharaoh, or a lusty priest.

Perhaps in this life I am actually a slayer of hearts, even though nobody knows it yet. Maybe I am meant to be pursued by Kathy Ireland, Naomi Campbell, and Cindy Crawford all at once. It's only that they've never happened by the Starlight Lanes in Cincinnati on a Friday night and seen me in action.

Out of five billion human beings on this planet, there is only one me, perhaps because the world isn't big enough for two. My insights and opinions are worth as much as the next man's, probably even more. I could write a novel or not. I could host my own successful television talk show. Who knows what awesome destiny I am meant to fulfill.

I'm special just because I'm me. My mom said so.

MATURITY/SOPHISTICATION

I'm extremely careful. I've never turned blue in someone else's bathroom. I consider that the height of bad manners.

Keith Richards

Face it, one man's sushi is another man's fish bait. So you'd much rather go have an egg in the skillet at the Short Stop than chateaubriand at Laffite's. So you'd rather watch football than have sex with your wife. So she insists you look stupid in leather fringe. She's not exactly Sharon Stone, either.

How often we are told that we're acting foolish, immature, or boorish because we don't fit someone else's narrow-minded definition of sophistication or maturity? But this is because we're rebels, unappreciated trailblazers who do not fear the disapproval of the cultural elite or the culturally bankrupt.

We know there's nothing worth watching on PBS. We know it doesn't matter what we eat or how we eat it; it all winds up in the same place eventually. Well, more or less. And hey, Road Runner is still the funniest damn thing on TV and we're not afraid to admit it.

If my inner child says it's cool, it's cool. End of discussion.

HOSTING/BUSYNESS

Every man likes the smell of his own farts.

Icelandic proverb

Whenever I have visitors, I find myself so busy playing the good host that I forget to enjoy their company. I forget that they came over to see me, not to sit on a chair or drink beer out of a glass. This is unfortunate, because as I have neither furniture nor drinking glasses, sometimes I can get to feeling pretty bad about my hospitality.

I've got to remember that being close to somebody means letting them feel right at home. That's why I've started to allow Mom to stop by and clean the oven, as long as she closes the kitchen door while she's going it, because those fumes can be carcinogenic and cause birth defects in future generations. Mom's already had all her kids, but she ought to be more considerate about my reproductive capabilities. After all, I'm still a young man.

I can hear her murmuring to herself contentedly, and when she emerges, flushed with enthusiasm, I know she's pleased that I've given her the chance to express her love for me and to be at home in my world.

Next month, maybe I'll give her a big kick and rent a carpet steam cleaner. I'll probably have to get a hotel room for myself that weekend, though. Those things are known to cause tumors in lab rats.

BALANCE/RESPONSIBILITIES

I have a tendency to get really drunk and then I get to the hotel and I'll pick the first chick that I can get. . . . You'd be surprised at some of the chicks I've picked up. . . . What you do is you go up to the room and just drink till they look good.

Slash

Okay, okay, so I screwed up. It's not like I meant to call her Anne instead of Shirley. It just slipped out. And it's not like I intentionally forgot to bring a condom. So I forgot to mention that I'm married. It's an understandable omission, given the heat of the moment.

What can I say? I'm a whimsical, impetuous kind of a guy. I'm fun loving and free. I'm a live wire.

So occasionally I slip up on the minor details. I forget to cross my *t*'s and dot my *i*'s. I miss a few deadlines and cut a few corners when it comes to annoying details like health, hygiene, income taxes, and federal regulations governing the use of controlled substances. I'm worth it.

I'd rather be fun than done.

TRAVEL

A good traveler is one who does not know where he is going.
                                                        Lin Yutang

What a thrill it is when the world stretches before us like an open highway! What a sensation to go where no man has gone before, or at least never when he was sober.

Men are born explorers. Women sometimes think that they are explorers, too, but it is best to discourage them from subscribing to this theory because they may get ideas about coming along and spoiling the fun.

Our explorations take many forms. We may take a road trip across town to the new go-go joint on the county line. We may test the limits of our boss's patience or the grace period on our auto insurance.

Whatever the territory, we Men Who Do Next to Nothing must not shrink from boldly probing into unknown nooks and crannies.

If Columbus had listened to his wife and gotten a real job, he never would have discovered America.

BEAUTY

When I'm in the studio and I'm creating beauty, I'm six foot nine and look like Cary Grant. And then I see that reduced to this nebbishy little guy with a double chin.

Billy Joel

When I get to feeling badly about my success with the babes, I remind myself that Christie Brinkley married Billy Joel. She has great legs. I try to imagine myself surrounded by legs: long legs; short legs; legs with chubby knees connected to ripe, fleshy little thighs; or bony knees, blending gracefully into long, lush thighs that seem to go all the way up to her belly button . . . and beyond. . . .

I usually start to feel a lot better when I realize that legs are a large part of my life. Not only the gams on the babe in the Purchasing department but other gams, on other babes, in other departments, in other buildings, in other cities all across the country.

When I get discouraged, I remind myself that there is beauty before, behind, below, and if I'm lucky, even above me.

Boots were made for more than just walking.

TRUTH

Pay no attention to the truth.

Jules Renard

We live in a dishonest society. Everybody lies: politicians, businessmen, the bartender who says he's out of those little pigs in blankets even though Happy Hour is only half over. In business, in politics, and in bars, it seems the successful communicator is the one who can talk the best game, regardless of whether or not he's telling the truth. The prize goes to the best bullshitter.

Clearly, our world is more concerned with winning than truth telling, and as Men Who Do Next to Nothing, we have learned that to try to fight fairly, to point out that we should have been alerted to the pigs in blankets shortage before being poured our fourth Johnnie Walker, gets us nowhere. Still, we argue with ourselves until we are so exhausted that we cannot stay awake long enough to catch *Muffy Goes to Boarding School* on the Playboy channel. Maybe we should learn that in this world we are going to have to bend a little, and if a guy twice our size tells us he's out of pigs in blankets, we're just going to have to settle for a chili dog at Cow Chip Charlie's.

The truth hurts, but so does Scotch on an empty stomach.

SECRETS

No one needs to know anything.

Jean Paul

The 12 Step program teaches that we are as sick as the secrets we keep. Secrets are like an acid eating away at ourselves and our relationships. When we keep a secret we sacrifice a piece of ourselves, and ultimately we are devoured, thread by thread, very much like an edible sheet.

An essential ingredient of recovery is to give up our secrets and live our lives in the open. Let your neighbors see you sleeping in the hammock at noon on a Tuesday. Those sneers are probably just because they're jealous. Let them see you taking a leak in your bushes. It's your hedge, and it looks damn healthy. Let your lawn grow. Don't shave. Don't change your shirt for a week. Refuse to shower. These are the outer manifestations of the inner man and should be displayed proudly like a medal of honor, not hidden beneath a well-manicured exterior, cowering beneath layers of pima cotton and Aramis for men.

The French say, "He who eats sheets before bedtime wakes up with cotton mouth."

SATISFACTION

I can't hardly sing, you know what I mean? I'm no Tom Jones and I don't give a fuck.

Mick Jagger

Sometimes satisfaction seems unattainable. Yet to be satisfied with ourselves is like a warm Jacuzzi with the jets angled just so. It is so peaceful and cleansing to be truly content with who we are and where we are at this moment.

Often, we equate contentment and satisfaction with stagnation. This is absolutely true, and when this occurs to us we must congratulate ourselves for being on the right track.

After all, which is more peaceful, a still pond or a rushing stream? Can anything truly be said to grow in white water? Can fish eat lunch in it?

Satisfaction is a stagnant pond of quietude, a lunch break from the rapids of life, but it gets kind of crowded at the noon hour, so make your reservations early.

Men, like algae, flourish in standing water.

MALE BONDING

One's friends are that part of the human race with which one can be human.

George Santayana

One of the devastating consequences of the constant and hectic froth of activity in our lives is that we have less and less contact with our friends. Friendship is a time for letting our hair down, for reveling in the differences and similarities that have drawn and kept us together. Friendship is a time to remember common histories and to be young bucks frolicking in the fields once more.

When did you last spend time with a friend? Can you even remember the last time you went to a hot-oil wrestling match or hung out on a street corner with a pal, smoking cigarettes and discussing automobiles, women, and condom sizes, not necessarily in that order?

What a shame that as employed adults we have placed work over friendship and have come to treat our friends the way our wives treat us—kind of like stale bread that we haven't gotten around to making into croutons yet.

Strike a blow for brotherhood. Organize a circle jerk.

WONDER

He's intercepted the ball at the forty-five-yard line. He's bro-
ken away, ten, thirty, forty-five yards for the touchdown.
He's really earned his twelve point five million today.

John Madden

I hear the above passage, and I feel lost in wonder at the beauty of athletic competition. As I listen, I envision a brisk fall afternoon, cold beer, and bleachers. I can hear the roar of the crowd and glimpse the cartwheeling cheerleaders in those cute little pleated numbers, with their thighs pink from the cold, straining against gravity as they hurl themselves heavenward; up and up they go, along with their skirts and those cute little cropped sweaters that play peekaboo with me and everyone else in the first four rows.

I wonder at the grace and command of the quarterback, the salaries these guys make, and all the poontang they must nail.

At moments like this, the workaday world seems far away, which is where it belongs.

Wonder is a gift of real living—real living is a gift of the NFL.

SELF-LOVE

Self-love, my liege, is not so vile a sin as self-neglecting.
William Shakespeare

We are so accustomed to doing what others want us to do, or doing what is right, or doing what earns us money, that we have lost touch with our inner selves. We have grown so used to listening to the "shoulds" that we can no longer hear the "would if we coulds." In the fight to meet our responsibilities, we have stopped knowing ourselves. We have denied our own needs and have come down with such a severe case of blue balls that we may never recover.

Imagine starting each day with the question, "What would I do today if I could?" What would be your answer? I'll give you a hint. It probably has nothing to do with getting out of bed and going to work. Just as an exercise, try shutting off that alarm clock. Try missing the 8:07. Try out that new pair of chamois gloves the girlfriend got you for Christmas.

Try to visualize what your inner self is saying. If you're like the rest of us Men Who Do Next to Nothing, it's probably saying, "Jeez, why didn't I think of these gloves before?"

Do they make Playtex gloves for men?

SELF-ESTEEM/SELF-ABUSE

Of course we revel in our own fucking genius. Why the hell not? Self-indulgence is what we're full of and we're proud of it.

Johnny Rotten (Lydon)

Our feelings of unworthiness often lead us to abuse ourselves. One of the most common forms of self-abuse is work. Another is marriage. Many Men Who Do Next to Nothing are beginning to see that it is abusive to the self to keep so busy that we have no time to experience those things in life that make us feel good, like forests, or sunsets, or wet T-shirt nights at the Hell Hole.

It is abusive to the self to be so busy taking care of others that we neglect our own needs. And when we are unkind to ourselves it is inevitable that we will be unkind to others, which is an excellent argument for not visiting your in-laws. Try it out next Thanksgiving.

Although self-abuse is okay for some people, I do not believe that it is right for me.

HELPLESSNESS

Sitting is better than standing, lying is better than sitting.
Indian proverb

Me? Helpless? An empty skid on the loading dock of life? You bet! Is this bad? I don't think so. I know that when I struggle to achieve and succeed, I feel ragged around the edges, my personal life takes a beating, and all I end up with for my pains is a paycheck eaten up by the government, interest payments, and dial 900-HOT-BABE.

Maybe I need to accept my helplessness, my utter lack of control over my own success or failure, and realize that if my life does need something, it'll turn up eventually, and if it doesn't, I probably didn't need it anyway.

Just finding a reason to get up in the morning is enough of a challenge. What was that 900 number again?

INTIMACY/ISOLATION

If it weren't for pickpockets I'd have no sex life.
Rodney Dangerfield

Human beings were not made to live in isolation. If we were, there would be no such thing as stadium concerts with festival seating. I like to get close, real close, to my fellow human beings. Women, I mean. I find that a bus at rush hour is a great place to achieve intimacy. So they usually don't look as good as Barbara Dare, but they have one thing going for them. They're three-dimensional.

It's just not enough to watch all the time. Sometimes I have to get involved, as long as that involvement is confined to the eight-block stint on the crosstown express.

I deserve a soul mate. I deserve two. Preferably at the same time.

NEEDS/DESIRES

I've looked on a lot of women with lust.

Jimmy Carter

Have you ever heard a fog horn? It's that low and mournful sound, penetrating the mist, leading blind ships ashore. For me, that baritone wail sounds the depths of despair and puts me in mind of the desolation of the human heart when it hasn't gotten laid in a month and a half.

When I feel despairing and alone, caught in the heavy grayness of my existence, I find that duplicating the sounds of the fog horn can lead me safely to shore. I groan, I whine, I howl into the night, and before you know it, light appears in the midst of my murkiness, red flashing lights, coming to find out who is making all the racket in 2B.

In the stillness I can hear the sound of my needs demanding to be met. So can my neighbors.

FEAR

A man who has learned not to feel fear will find the fatigue of daily life enormously diminished.

Bertrand Russell

Fear is often the first link in a chain of emotions that can lead to activity. Fear can make us do all sorts of exhausting things. Fear makes us put our tails between our legs or hang our heads in shame. A final warning at work leads us at last to write up those reports that were due six months ago. An ultimatum from our wife or girlfriend spurs us to run to the nearest jeweler and pop for some overpriced bauble. All needless, fear-motivated activity.

We must learn to suppress our fears before they lead us to actions that embarrass us. When we feel that familiar knot beginning to form in the pit of our stomach, we must ignore it and wait for it to go away. It's bound to eventually. And if it doesn't, pound a fistful of Tums and forget about it.

What's wrong with repression? It works.

EXPECTATIONS

Blessed is the man who expects nothing, for he shall never be disappointed.

Alexander Pope

Expectations are the worst! They are setups for disappointment and misunderstanding, particularly when other people are expecting something from us.

Many a pleasant evening has been sacrificed at the altar of expectation. Remember last Friday night when you took that fox from Purchasing out for Chinese, after which you expected to take her home and test out your edible sheets, but before this she expected to discuss the future of your relationship? What was the result? Disappointment? Misunderstanding? Certainly nobody was biting any sheets that night.

Be alert to the dangers of expectations. The next time she expects a relationship, or even dinner, explain to her that expectations are an illusion of control, which ought to be stamped out before being allowed to screw up another Friday night.

When we are tied to expectations, we usually don't get laid. Besides, who needs dinner when you've got edible sheets?

NATURE/MASCULINITY

Like, peace and love, motherfucker, or you're gonna die! I'm gonna kick your ass if you fuck with my garden.

Axl Rose

Deep down inside each of us is a wild man, a guttural, visceral, irascible being who if turned loose would call in sick tomorrow morning and see who is on *Live with Regis & Kathie Lee*.

Who is this wild man, this virile beast within, who bays at the moon and at girls wearing those thong things? Could this possibly be me? God, I hope so.

Imagine a world where your wild man can roam free as the tide, where you don't have to hide, where you can live as free as the wind, unfettered by the expectations of others, or condoms. Imagine a world where beauty surrounds you, where women take you to dinner and then expect something in return. Imagine that you are born free.

Wild men, like lions, need nothing more than a grassy knoll and a large plain tree to be utterly fulfilled.

FREEDOM

Bo bo bo b'do bo . . .

The Cream

Addiction to activity is a progressive disease, which, if allowed to fester unattended, can rob us of our reason and even our enjoyment of life. We begin innocently enough, changing a light bulb, mending a roof leak, and the next thing we know projects like cleaning the gunk caked up around the base of the toilet or scrubbing petrified bits of food clinging to the walls of the sink begin to suggest themselves. Consider this: Would we have even seen the gunk or the petrified bits if we had not changed that light bulb in the first place?

We must embrace the freedom that exists in the semidarkness. We must recognize the inherent threat to our being in that first step toward doing. We must cast off the chains of guilt and duty that bind us and recognize that we are free men, if we choose to be.

Freedom's just another word for nothing left to do.

ACTION

He who acts, spoils; he who grasps, lets slip.

Lao-tse

If there is anything we Men Who Do Next to Nothing have learned in our recovery, it's how to avoid getting things done. We have become experts at avoidance. We have an unswerving instinct for looking in the opposite direction whenever things need to be done. It's a way of life and one we are proud of.

Sometimes, though, we forget to celebrate how important our practical, everyday avoidances are. We long for some monumental task to shirk, some huge, all-important oversight. Yet our lives are made up of ordinary chores that need to be ignored: getting to work every morning, paying the bills, fixing the furnace. These common, routine avoidances can seem small and insignificant, yet they are not as meaningless as they might seem, as you will find out next winter, so we must remember to recognize them.

If they cut off my heat, my pipes will burst, which means I won't have to bathe anymore. There is a positive side to everything, if we look in the right place.

FOOLISH BEHAVIOR

A fool has a fine world.

Yiddish proverb

The harder we strive to avoid working, the more flak we take from the unenlightened majority who actually think that work is important. We Men Who Do Next to Nothing know that although the grasshopper and the ant lead very different lives—one a creature of leisure, the other a creature of endless toil—they come to the same end, either squashed under somebody's boot or fried by a kid with a magnifying glass. So why work so hard? Why work at all?

So some people call us fools. Why? Because we don't have a six-figure salary, a stock portfolio, or furniture in our apartment? But while we're gorging on Little Debbie cakes and perusing the new swimsuit edition, what are all those wise guys doing? They're working. So we must ask ourselves: Who is the fool, and who is the wise man?

What good is furniture if you're too busy to sit on it?

COMPETITION

Nice guys finish last.

Leo Durocher

May the best man win. Sounds fair, unless of course you're not the best man. What if you're the second-best guy, or the third or the fourth? What if you're not even in the wedding party?

What if we don't have an uncle on the board of directors, a friend who is sleeping with the professor, or a girlfriend with a mortgage? What if we are underemployed? What if, in the race of life, we are saddled with lead Nikes?

The point is, when we stop worrying about winning races, these things don't matter. We no longer have to compare ourselves with that jerk down the hall who takes his girlfriend to the Bahamas twice a year and still has enough left over to not only pay rent, but purchase Minoxidil on a regular basis.

Besides, we've got a lot to offer when we think about it. How about that belching thing or our 10 percent employee discount on recreational rifles? That's pretty good.

I'm doing the best I can, and that's all that really matters.

PROCESS

I can't be forced to do anything.

Sid Vicious

Process. I instinctively cringe when I hear that word. I imagine myself plodding along in endless toil toward some long-term abstract goal, like death.

But process is simply a term for the way we do things, like washing only the tops of our dinner plates. I mean, that's the side you eat off of, right? Why wash the bottoms? Or like walking the dog at night so you don't have to scoop the poop. What are they gonna do? Dust for fingerprints?

When our processes help us save time, money, or, more important, precious personal energy resources, they are invaluable. Take a moment today to cut a new corner. Drink straight from the milk carton of life and leave the refrigerator door open while you're doing it.

The shortest distance between two points is usually a creative maneuver, best done out of the sight of a police officer.

PURPOSE/MEANING/
FEELING NEEDED

Act if you like, but do it at your peril.

Ralph Waldo Emerson

So often the world places a high premium on being needed, being useful, and having a purpose. Things that do not meet these rigid criteria are tossed away, dismissed, discarded, donated to a local charity, or left to languish in the back of the fridge until they ferment into food for cockroaches—unless your ex-mother-in-law decides to come over for dinner, in which case you'll cut off the blue stuff and serve it to her on toast.

Are we to become fodder for lower life forms before our time? No! This is why it is so very important to keep breathing and have a detectable pulse at all times, even when in a turkey-and-football coma.

We must also remember that life is its own justification. Like the cockroach, we are our own very special link in the food chain, and it's going to take more than boric acid to stop us from following our natural instincts.

Between the past and the present, I am the missing link.

EMPTINESS

We all remember, don't we? That terrible moment when we looked around and realized, This is it. This is the end of the road, the final frontier, the whole shooting match. This is my life, my home, my woman, my inferior stereo system. This is all I'll ever be, do, have, and let's face it, it's been a downhill slide since high school. I'm just another nobody, a dust mote in the cosmic scheme of things, a zero, a bum, a loser.

But then it hit us, didn't it? Like a blast of fresh air on a clear adolescent autumn afternoon with a dog and a brew and a whole squad of sweet-thighed high school cheerleaders crying out our name 'cause we just aced the big game against those meatballs from Central.

In that moment of despair, we suddenly remembered that the new Kim Basinger movie is on HBO in twenty minutes and that Domino's Pizza delivers.

Attitude adjustment is a lot easier than life adjustment.

DISAPPOINTMENT

Have the neighborhood kids been right all along? Am I truly nothing?

Al Bundy

Disappointment. Remorse. Regret for the roads not taken. When these feelings of sadness and insecurity overwhelm us, we begin to reassess the decisions we have made in life and to reflect upon what might have been had we chosen differently.

Maybe it is a good idea to really experience the depth of regret lying fallow in our stagnant minds. Maybe we ought to lie down to get the full effect. Once we are lying down, though, and the couch pillow is supporting our neck just so, holding our gaze in perfect alignment with the fifty-yard line while maintaining our mouth at enough of an angle to be able to sip out of a can without raising our head, we feel validated. We remember why we have chosen to be Men Who Do Next to Nothing and remember, too, that regret is something that women invented to make men go to work every day.

As we let ourselves experience our grief and pain, particularly when we experience it at a 180-degree angle, it all begins to feel like something else, something along the lines of euphoria.

When life gets you down, lie down. What's the point in fighting gravity?

CONTENTMENT

We are happy from possessing what we like, not from possessing what others like.

La Rochefoucauld

Happiness is an elusive and spontaneous thing. Often we fool ourselves into thinking that if we had a better handle on our lives—if, for instance, we had a nice car, a better job, or some idea of how we were going to pay the rent next month—then we would be happy. Of course, when we actually do pay the rent we feel depressed because we've thrown all that money out the window for some cheap dump right next door to an old bat who calls the cops every time you turn up your stereo above level five. What a witch. Then we wonder why we can never feel contentment or happiness. We wonder where we have gone wrong.

The first mistake we made was in listening to the woman who told us that we'd feel better once we had a better job and could pay our bills. These material things don't bring us happiness. Happiness cannot be planned or purchased. Maybe it's time we begin to question the woman who taught us that possessions and power can bring us contentment. Maybe she owes us a six-pack for dishing out such rotten advice. Come to think of it, it may be the same woman who keeps calling the cops. Something should be done about her.

Happiness comes from within, and occasionally from Anheuser-Busch.

SUCCESS

Success has ruined many a man.

Benjamin Franklin

Perhaps it isn't success itself but the way in which we define it that causes us so many problems. If we define success as having a job, a house, or a car with a functional transmission, then we are bound to feel like losers.

If, on the other hand, we say that success is the ability to live healthy, contented lives, or if, for instance, we define success as getting through a day without suffocating or getting mugged on the subway, how much more comfortable would we be with ourselves?

Starting today, I'm going to learn to be happy with each and every accomplishment and reward myself accordingly. When I wake up and get out of bed tomorrow, first I'm going to congratulate myself and then, as a reward, I'm going to lie right back down. I could go on like that for weeks.

I am as successful as I think I am.

TRAVEL

The soul of a journey is liberty . . .

William Hazlitt

One of our strong points as Men Who Do Next to Nothing is our understanding of the value of vacations in the process of recovery. Vacations mean a break in routine, a time of rest and renewal, a time to pamper ourselves. When we travel, we open ourselves up to new experiences, new women, new athletic teams, and different kinds of beers on tap. The change in scenery vacuums out the cobwebs of monotony, restores our spirit, and makes us feel brand spanking new. Which reminds me of that weekend in Tijuana. But that was a different kind of spanking, although I did feel new afterward.

How sad that we must relegate this expansive experience to a mere two weeks out of each year. How weary and irritable we become with the dull routine of our lives. Perhaps it is time to ask ourselves some difficult questions. Isn't it time to look into taking a permanent vacation? Shouldn't we be looking into how unemployment benefits work? Couldn't we get by on her salary?

Vacations don't have to be expensive. Cerveza's dirt cheap in Tijuana.

If I buy a case of Dos Equis, maybe I could have a vacation right here on my couch.

HIGHER POWER

One with God is a majority.

Adam Clayton Powell

How easy it is to forget that our Higher Power is always there to give us strength and courage. How else would we find the courage to say, "No! I will not go to the store just to buy toilet paper. If I can do without it, so can she!" Where else can we find the inner strength to say, "Yes! I like the grayish half-light created by the soot caked to my window, and I will not clean it off."

When we are in touch with our Higher Power, we see the Zen-like beauty in all things. Like that pile of old papers and empty Roach Motel boxes on top of the VCR. Is it garbage? Is it art? Certainly it's worth thinking about for a few more weeks.

When we are in touch with our Higher Power we know what we are about and can stand up to those who question our priorities, like our bosses, who place budget meetings over office football pools, or our friends, who think we should pay them the fifty bucks we owe them before springing for a new pair of Ray-Bans.

When we are truly one with our Higher Power, we are at peace, we are cool, we are credible, and best of all we are probably unemployed.

I wouldn't want to mess with God's will.

LONELINESS

Solitude would be ideal if you could pick the people to avoid.
Karl Kraus

It's funny, but even when we are surrounded by people, we can find ourselves feeling alone, separated from the rest of mankind, out of place, and out of the loop.

We need to share special moments of connection with others. We need to feel we are not alone in thinking there's a big difference between Miller Lite and Genuine Draft. We need to know that someone else thinks the "Trouble with Tribbles" *Star Trek* episode is overrated. We need to be comforted that someone else understands the devastating ramifications of instant replay and truly needs his MTV.

When we feel lonely we must reach out. Wouldn't it be nice to share our most intimate thoughts with that hot A&P checkout girl with the awesome pair of cupcakes?

Today, I will not dwell on my feelings of aloneness. I will make new friends and keep the old, for one is silver and the other gold.

Reach out and touch someone. Just be sure you can't get arrested for it.

TOIL

[W]e have toiled all the night, and have taken nothing. . . .

Luke 5:5

This quotation is so aptly reflective of the ultimate emptiness of the oppressive system of enforced labor in which we live. It is a system subtly imposed by women and one we have learned to conform to in order to get laid.

This is not reality, it is a conspiracy, perpetrated by workaholic women and perpetuated by us helpless addicts who would do anything in exchange for the wild thing.

Fortunately, if we are courageous, there are other options. and not all of them cause blindness.

One in the hand is worth two in the office.

HOUSEWORK

A good housewife is of necessity a humbug.

W. M. Thackeray

They say there are two inevitabilities in life: death and taxes. Taxes, though, are easily avoided—just refuse to work. And death doesn't worry me much because it only happens once, and it doesn't cost money. But there is a third inevitable curse that they habitually forget to mention: housework.

No matter how many times you clean, you always have to do it again. As an experiment, I tried to get around the fruitlessness of housework by living nude in an empty apartment and eating all my meals out. But one morning, lying naked on the floor in my sanctuary, I saw it—dust on my baseboards, dust on my light fixtures, dust on the floors and windowsills. There was even dust on me. That fateful morning I realized that no matter where you go, there is always going to be dust. There is no lint-free corner to retreat to, no place where you are completely safe from housework.

That is the day I decided to move in with my girlfriend.

A woman's work is never done, so what difference will a few more loads of laundry make?

CHANGE

I must accept that no matter how hard I try, some things will never change. In fact, most things won't. My salary, for instance, my future prospects, that rattling in the radiator of my Pontiac, male-pattern balding. It's a discouraging list.

Of course another thing I can't change is that some things are going to change, like my marital status, which has proved extremely mercurial, as has my place of employment. My TRS report is in constant flux. Sometimes nightmares that look just like good opportunities come my way and change my bank balance.

Let's face it: changing or not changing, it's all one giant, miasmic, disastrous, infinitely collapsible world in which a guy is better off just grabbing a pillow and ducking for cover.

If opportunity knocks, don't answer the door. Let her get it.

POWER

Power without abuse loses its charm.

Paul Valéry

As we begin to recover, to get in touch with our true selves and to accept who we genuinely are, we begin to get the idea that we may in fact be all-powerful beings.

We begin to sense that awesome power first in relation to others, like when we scream at our families, neighbors, co-workers, or employers. Next we are screaming at whole teams of guys much larger than us on the television, and soon we are screaming at large institutions, like the Department of Motor Vehicles, or the Office of Unemployment, or even the entire U.S. government, but usually only over the telephone. The government can't afford caller ID.

Gradually we begin to feel that power glowing and radiating within ourselves. We uncover the Spartan warrior within us, standing our ground at Thermopylae, combing our luxuriant locks in calm defiance of the invading Athenians. We flex, we grimace, we don't change our underwear for a week.

Today, I will assert my power. After all, I'm a taxpayer. At least in theory.

RELATIONSHIPS/ COMMITMENTS

Promises and pie-crust are made to be broken.
Jonathan Swift

Our fathers thought they had it all figured out. Get a good job, and you get a good woman. Take care of her financially, and she'll take care of you physically and emotionally. What this amounts to is that for a little chicken soup during flu season, clean shirts, and an occasional (very occasional, to hear my father tell it) afternoon quickie, our fathers allowed themselves to become success objects.

We modern Men Who Do Next to Nothing have other options. Modern morality makes it possible for us to escape the success trap. People live with each other now before getting married; women work. These new advances in gender relations can be used to our advantage. There are women out there who, in exchange for an occasional Hallmark card and a few vague references to future commitment, will contribute to our lives not only emotionally and physically, but financially as well.

Never say "I do" when you can get away with "I might."

CONFUSION

Lack of understanding is a great power. Sometimes, it enables men to conquer the world.

Anatole France

So often, we Men Who Do Next to Nothing are expected to be rational. Yet so much of our life just doesn't make sense. When we struggle for logic and clarity, we get confused and irritable. We become the kind of man who kicks small animals, becomes a nuisance at cocktail parties, and demands to know things like how bombs can be called peacekeepers or what the purpose of monogamy is in an overpopulated world.

In our recovery, we have learned that no matter how hard we try, nothing is going to make sense. We can't understand what's going on because invariably women are involved somewhere in the process, and they remain one of life's eternal riddles.

If you don't know an answer, skip it and go on to the next question.

COURTESY

Good manners are made up of petty sacrifices.
                                    Ralph Waldo Emerson

We Men Who Do Next to Nothing are constantly feeling the pressure to be nice, to be courteous, to mind our manners and do our fair share. Many of us have given in to this restrictive mandate and have experimented with politeness. We found out that being polite is not only dishonest and detrimental to our recovery, but a lot of unnecessary effort that doesn't pay off in the long run.

Those of us trying to get clearer with ourselves must face the fact that courtesy is a deception. Real men don't really say "Excuse me." They don't write thank-you notes. They don't volunteer to help with the dishes. They don't get up and leave the room when they have to fart. So why lie to ourselves and those close to us?

If we want to be honest with ourselves and others, we have to be willing to let go of niceness along with excess intestinal gas.

COMPARISON

Comparisons are always odious and ill taken.
Miguel de Cervantes

How beautiful and joyful it is to accept ourselves the way that we truly are. How sad that women so often have difficulty appreciating the purity of our visceral selves. How unfortunate that they must always compare us with others, like Arnold Schwarzenegger, Donald Trump, or the guy next door with a full-time job.

Held to impossibly high standards, of course we don't measure up. We are too short, too tall, too fat, too passive, too underemployed. But to compare human beings is to miss out on the unique splendor of each individual. Who else could name from memory every RBI in Babe Ruth's final season? And not just anybody could drink forty-seven kamikazes without blowing chunks. All these are indeed special gifts.

Imagine a day—today, for example—when you express your unique splendor and are appreciated. Go ahead, demonstrate that trick with the shot glass and the condom.

UNITY/ONENESS

All for one, one for all.

Alexandre Dumas

Part of our disease is thinking that it is up to us to do something about our situation in life and that we are all alone in a cold and unfriendly universe. What a relief to reassure ourselves that our Higher Power, our wife, or some significant other is there to take control and sort out our dirty from our clean, our whites from our brights, our dry cleaning from our hand washables. What a serene pleasure to know that we just have to sit back and let it happen.

When we recognize that the forces outside of ourselves are actually much better at this sort of thing than the force within, we begin to heal. When a man realizes that his mate is merely an extension of himself, a more capable extension that never fades his colors, then he can sit back, turn the showerhead to massage, and revel in the unity of the universe.

Healing is the experience of the oneness of all things. Therefore, in a unified universe, my mate is the same as myself, so if she goes to work, then so do I, even though I'm at the arcade playing air hockey.

What is mine is hers, so let her wash it.

FEELINGS

Feel slightly, think little, never plan.

Benjamin Disraeli

So often we are told that we must express our feelings in order to be modern men. This is a twofold dilemma. First, we must actually have these feelings, and then, as if that weren't enough, we are supposed to talk about them.

At the urging of our significant others, we have attended weekend seminars, therapy sessions, relationship classes, couples retreats, and 12 Step meetings. We've tried to tap into, get in touch with, embrace, cherish, and communicate our innermost feelings. Why is it at these times we are unable to communicate that the strongest emotion we feel is irritation that we must get in touch with deep-seated emotions we don't have?

This is a lot of effort in the service of self-deception. Today, if someone asks you "How are you feeling?" tell them you are feeling absolutely nothing. Even if this isn't entirely true, insist upon it anyway. You'll save a fortune in therapy bills and keep your weekends free for the only effective mental medicine yet invented, Saturday afternoon football and a case of Bud.

Denial ain't just a river in Egypt.

TRANSITION/STABILITY

Any very great and sudden change is death.

Samuel Butler

There is no hiding from the fact that transition is traumatic. Change feels like a direct, personal attack because, very often, it is.

Remember last week when your favorite plaid velour chair that you've loved ever since you stole it from outside Vito's Calzone King to put in your dorm room had simply vanished? And for what reason? Because she thinks it's ugly? Because she doesn't care if it is comfortable, it still clashes with the carpet? Because she's got connections down at the Salvation Army and can get next day, curbside pickup service?

No! It's because you moved in with your girlfriend. You changed your place of residence. It's because change means movement, transformation, readjustment. Change means work, and work means getting up out of that favorite chair, leaving it vulnerable to diabolical designers who would color-coordinate your comfort right out of existence.

If it isn't broken, don't fix it. In fact, even if it is broken, don't bother. It's fine the way it is.

SECRETS

He who tells the truth should have one foot in the stirrup.

Arab proverb

Our current culture instructs us that only total honesty will pave the way to intimacy. This is because the culture is currently being manipulated by women who don't know what's good for them.

They don't really want to know where you were last Wednesday night. And when she asks you if you think she's getting fat, there's only one right answer.

Let's face it, truth is not always the best solution. If women were really being honest with us and themselves, they wouldn't ask questions that they already know the answers to just to trick us into saying something that's going to make them feel morally justified in withholding sex for two weeks.

In reality, confessions are best entrusted to priests, bartenders, and, if a large payment is involved, the tabloids. After all, if you're rich, you can buy intimacy.

I refuse to answer on the grounds that I may incriminate myself.

WORK/RELATIONSHIPS

Work is the curse of the drinking classes.

Oscar Wilde

Why are women always objectifying things? Why do they make so many demands on us? And what is all this nonsense about relationships being work? I mean, every time you see her lately she has another reference to some form of enforced relationship labor, and she was the one who insisted on calling what was a perfectly good casual fling a relationship in the first place. There's emotional work, personal work, inner work. There's work to share more of yourself, express your inner feelings. There's being-somewhat-less-of-a-lazy-son-of-a-bitch-and-get-up-off-the-couch-while-you're-at-it-and-vacu-um-something work and, of course, the ever-popular you-should-appreciate-me-more work.

This is not what you planned on when you caught that first look at her in Purchasing and asked her out for Chinese. This was not what you went through twelve pairs of edible sheets for. If you wanted to work, you would have kept your job. At least you got paid twice a month and had your weekends and holidays free.

If a relationship was meant to be work, they'd have to pay you to be in one.

ENTHUSIASM

Enthusiasm is very wearing.

Robert Louis Stevenson

Several weeks ago, I made a fundamental decision for myself. I decided that I would do only work that I was enthusiastic about. Since then I have been unemployed.

I was a barrel reamer in a munitions plant then. I decided not to ream any barrels about which I was unenthusiastic. I would not put in any hours, sweep any metal shavings, or oil any pistons just because of the money.

I resolved that I would only do things that put me in touch with myself, like reading magazines in the men's room, or watching the babe in Purchasing bend over to pick up the pencils I dropped by her desk. After I got fired, I decided to devote myself exclusively to those things that seemed related to the meaning and purpose of my life, like watching television or judging bikini contests or napping frequently.

I feared I would end up a derelict. I feared I would starve. Thank goodness she has a job.

ATTITUDE/PERCEPTION

We don't give a shit about inner attitude, just as long as it sounds good.

Johnny Rotten (Lydon)

I have spent the major portion of my life feeling like an empty bucket, a skinny pig, a barren field, a troutless stream. In fact, for most of my adult life, a good chunk of my childhood, and all of my adolescence, I've felt completely auxiliary to life.

Fortunately, adulthood has brought its compensations. Whenever I find myself feeling empty, I remind myself I'm alive by throwing a temper tantrum. I find these outbursts to be a valuable release that rids me of excess emotional gas. And there's always something handy to get irate about: the leaky bathroom faucet, the pants your girlfriend didn't pick up at the cleaners, the price of tea in China.

After an explosion I feel valued, I feel feared, and best of all, I feel that good kind of tired.

I'm not really empty. Even my girlfriend tells me I'm full of it.

LOVE/FORGIVENESS

Love means not ever having to say you're sorry.
Erich Segal, Love Story

I like to think of love as one giant eraser, rubbing out all the suffering, sorrow, and ugliness between people.

When you love someone you see their scars as stars and rub until the beautiful surface that lies beneath the emotional scribbling of pain, shame, and blame shines through and you can see your own reflection. Like a weathered barn, a smooth piece of driftwood, a kitchen counter with perfect ring-shaped coffee stains, love makes everything seem beautiful.

I tried to explain this to my roommate last month when my rent check bounced, but unfortunately, to her, love is an indelible marker, you know, the kind that not even all-temperature Cheer or a nuclear holocaust can wipe out, so my love eraser didn't stand much of a chance.

I stood my ground. I told her that someone who really loved me would accept me for who I am, rubber checks and all. They would accept my inner child, my innocence, and my bad credit rating, but all she would accept was my key and a promise to have my things out by Monday.

I forgive myself for my past. I'm sure others will forgive me, too, and if they don't, I can move cross country, grow a beard, and get an unlisted phone number.

CARETAKING/PROVIDING

You'll be lucky to save your own ass, let alone somebody else's.
Axl Rose

In our diseased families of origin, we were told to eat our spinach and to drink our milk so we would grow up and be big strong men who could take care of our families. A fringe benefit, we were promised, was that we would be able to finally take care of the muscle-headed jerk on the beach who has been putting sand in our trunks since we were four.

Well, here we are, all grown up, and we aren't all Arnold Schwarzeneggers, are we? No. It all turned out to be just another deception, perpetrated by a generation of parents who all must have owned serious interest in the spinach industry.

As for taking care of our families, well, it's pretty hard to support a vice president of Purchasing in the style to which she is accustomed on a barrel reamer's salary. So I gave up.

I did cling to one goal, however. I am certain that with hard work and determination I can finally turn the tables on that muscle-headed jerk on the beach and dump a whole bucket full of sand down his trunks.

I will break the intergenerational chain of unrealistic expectations. I will never again eat spinach, and I am boycotting Popeye.

IMPRESSION MANAGEMENT

I despise making the most of one's time. Half of the pleasures of life consist of the opportunities one has neglected.
Oliver Wendell Holmes

I must. I should. I ought to. I damn well better. It's that stinkin' thinkin' again, telling us we aren't real men unless we behave like explorers or continent conquerors sailing the high seas of adventure, or at least the high seas of minimum wage employment.

That all sounds great on paper or in movies starring guys like Mel Gibson, who would actually look good in one of those pert little brimmed numbers with the red-and-white checkerboard bands and the buttons that say "Have It Your Way."

Taking risks calls for energy, a steel will, and good insurance coverage, none of which I have, so I try to stay home or as close to it as possible. Sticking my neck out and going on job interviews, traveling to places without a Burger King or cable, all cause more stress than I can deal with.

I have learned to push those "shoulds" right out of my mind. I'm no Indiana Jones, and that's just fine with me and Mutual of Omaha.

I'm into the modern mental machismo that doesn't require additional casualty insurance.

JOY

Yabba dabba do.

Fred Flintstone

Joy is spontaneous and unexpected. Joy cannot be planned for. It springs up and flowers on its own. What a comfort to realize that even if I never weed or water, I too can raise a crop of happiness.

What a relief to realize that we need not toil lovelessly for a mountain of materialistic mirth. We can just lie back and let joy happen. As long as we don't set our sights too high, joy will pop up unexpectedly and uncontrollably, like dandelions in a new lawn or like mushrooms on a cow pie.

Remember when that girl down the block that you've been in love with since you were twelve and suggested a game of strip Twister? Or remember when you called in sick and then realized there was a Three Stooges festival on TV and you hadn't even realized it before you called in? Remember when you discovered that you actually can put Tupperware in the dishwasher? What did you feel? Joy, right? Or at least something slightly more pleasant than the usual swift kick in the ass?

Next time you're thinking about shelling out the fifty bucks for a dozen roses to smell, smell a dandelion instead. They don't cost anything and require only minimal maintenance. Of course, they don't really smell, either, but what self-respecting man wants to smell a flower, anyway?

Given enough fresh compost, I can grow anything.

LEARNING

*His knowledge of books had in some degree diminished his
knowledge of the world.*

William Shenstone

I forgive myself for not reading. I used to feel kind of bad about it, but then I realized that life's most important lessons are not to be found in books.

Take my bullterrier, Pizzahead. Pizza taught me the sheer joy of beef by-products, telephone poles, and bitches in heat. Now that's what I call a life lesson. I can still see his little tail wagging as he made a beeline for the neighbor's poodle. God, that poodle was ripe. Her legs were shaved really close, except for two little balls at her hips and feet. And she had this pink bow cocked at a coquettish angle just above her lovely azure eyes.

Pizza taught me to love life, to forget about my responsibilities and just cut loose, ears flapping in the wind, stopping only to sniff at life's marvelous mysteries and relieve myself whenever I feel the need. I sure wish those guys who work at the state park could understand that.

Maybe if we stop thinking about education as something we find in books, we'll actually learn something.

The world is my classroom, my poodle, and my toilet.

WHOLENESS/UNITY

Life just is. You have to flow with it. Give yourself to the moment. Let it happen.

Governor Jerry Brown

We are all like fluid. We are off on a journey to our oceans of origin. All of us, ultimately, rejoin the universal wholeness from which we have sprung and to which we will return.

Some of us begin like crisp, sparkling champagne, others like day-old Coors. Ultimately we are all consumed by some poor, bleary-eyed slob trying to get a buzz on. We all proceed through this everyman's inner processes and are expelled once more into sewer systems that deposit us into rivers and streams whose swollen and degraded banks guide us safely back to our nascent seas.

Given the similarity between men and fluid, I would think twice about swimming in the ocean.

ESTEEM/COURAGE

There is no such thing as bravery, only degrees of fear.
John Wainwright

We're never good enough, are we? We're always looking for outside validation, believing we aren't worthy of feeling good about ourselves unless we live up to ridiculously high standards that have been set for us, like steady employment, retaining our driving privileges, or moving out of Mom and Dad's by the time we're forty.

We deserve a positive self-image regardless of our external accomplishments. So we still live at home and Mom still washes our socks and makes our beds every morning. So we don't have insurance, paid vacations, or a pension plan. So unemployment compensation has run out again. So the government is threatening to garnish wages we don't even earn anymore. Are these reasons for feeling like a loser?

We don't need to rescue people from burning buildings to feel like heroes. Waking up every morning with a will to survive takes a hell of a lot of courage.

I believe in a better tomorrow. I just prefer not to think that far ahead.

CONFLICT

It is a good rule in life never to apologize.

P. G. Wodehouse

Painful as it can be, conflict does sometimes arise. Of course, conflict takes a great deal of energy, and as we grow stronger in our conviction to do next to nothing, we must inevitably face the fact that this includes fighting, even if we are in the right.

We must always bear in mind that while conflict can be healthy (unless of course somebody is armed), there are easier, less tiring ways of getting our point across. We can reason our way to resolution. We can tell them the check is in the mail, the load is on the truck. We can tell them that we didn't mean anything by that last remark, some of our best friends are Polish. Spontaneous sleep is another option. It doesn't look good to hit a narcoleptic. Feigned drunkenness works. So does actual drunkenness. Pretend you've temporarily taken leave of your senses, lost your ability to swallow properly. Nobody wants to get drooled on just to make a point. The glasses thing doesn't work anymore, but nobody hits a blind man. There are always alternatives to conflict.

Peace on earth begins with me.

AGING/YOUTH

One of the things at my age is to avoid strain.

Arnold Bennett

I once met a guy in his fifties who shared with me what an awesome revelation it was when he discovered Grecian Formula for Men. "I can just lather and rinse," he told me, "and I don't have to deal with all that weird energy coming from babes who are old enough to be my wife."

Another guy in his forties told me that the way to stay young is to jog five miles a day. I have stopped returning his phone calls because I suspect that he has gone insane.

Why would anybody jog when they could just lather and rinse? It doesn't make sense. All that effort, and for what? Lower back and knee problems in later life, and it doesn't even change your hair color.

It seems to me that life is hard enough, what with breathing and bipedal locomotion and all, so why push it?

If man were meant to go three miles a day, he would have been born with a turbo engine.

BEAUTY/SELF-IMAGE

It is better to look good than to feel good.

Fernando

In our visually conscious culture, we feel the pressure to put aside those activities that give us pleasure because we are worried about looking good. We don't eat that sixth Twinkie, we forgo the family size bag of Doritos, because we are worried about our appearance.

We start to feel self-conscious when we compare ourselves to guys like Mel Gibson, Lawrence Taylor, or Jon Bon Jovi. We begin to dread looking in the mirror. We begin to measure ourselves against every guy on TV, computing in inches, in quarter inches, or in metric if it sounds bigger.

What we have to remember is that while women have to be beautiful, we Men Who Do Next to Nothing can rely on something called "character." We can be "distinguished" or "quirky," we can have loads of "personality," a big bank balance, or just enough room on our credit cards to make it look convincing.

Look at Keith Richards, Refrigerator Perry, Donald Trump. These are real men who are seeing major action in the trenches, and do you imagine that they are worried about an extra Twinkie here or there?

Dieting is for wimps. Does Dunkin' Donuts deliver?

RELATIONSHIPS

Relations stop nowhere.

Henry James

We Men Who Do Next to Nothing know more than we might think about healthy relationships. Even though most of our models for relationships are based on the unhealthy examples set by our dysfunctional parents, and even though our girlfriends have told us that we wouldn't know a good relationship if it came up and bit us on the butt, we have to realize that we have learned a thing or two about the endless opportunities available for new and better ways to relate to a whole variety of women.

Too often, relationships are looked at as some kind of eternal fix, like Super Glue. We are told that a relationship is a structure that gives form and shape to the bond between two people. Without it, we are like Jell-O without a mold. So what's wrong with putting Jell-O in other places, like in the bathtub, for example? Green Jell-O, about three hundred quarts of it, kept at room temperature, so it kind of squishes when you step into it and oozes into every available orifice and gets real interesting when you turn on the whirlpool jets, although this usually requires the presence of a competent plumber.

I'm Jell-O and you're glue. Whatever slides off me sticks to you. Sounds like fun.

JEALOUSY/LOST OPPORTUNITIES

Whenever a friend succeeds, a little something in me dies.
Gore Vidal

I admire a man who can own up to jealousy. It's an ugly emotion, and when we recognize ourselves turning green, we feel ashamed, particularly as it clashes with the couch.

It's only natural to resent those who have succeeded where we have failed, which means we Men Who Do Next to Nothing resent just about everybody, although only on alternate Thursdays because that much angst is just too exhausting on a daily basis.

It's hard to accept our station in life when we see where other guys are who have less on the ball than we do. I mean, can Schwarzenegger act? Can Dylan sing? No. And neither can we. So why aren't we making the same kind of money they are? It just isn't fair.

Nobody said life was fair, but I at least thought I was going to be graded on a curve.

PERSONAL SPACE/ GETTING AWAY

Unless we have a war or a big disease or a famine, there's just too many people, and they're gonna have to get off the planet.

Paul Kantner

Sometimes we just have to get away from everyone and everything to recharge our batteries. If we don't have a mountaintop retreat, or a summer home, since she got it in the divorce, we may have to find sanctuary elsewhere.

There are many spaces we can call our own. My favorite bat cave is the last booth at the Pleasure Chest. There I can get in touch with my inner self, my life force. As I slide in my fortieth quarter of the afternoon, I feel assured that there is a special place in the world just for me, and when you work it out, it comes to a lot less than the mortgage on that place in the Berkshires.

All I want is a room somewhere with a clap on, clap off light switch and a VCR.

GIVING CREDIT

He who believes in himself is always good.

Montesquieu

Do I devalue myself? Do I forget to give myself enough credit? Do I forget my positive qualities and focus only on the negative?

Today I will make a list of all that is good about me. I'm not on death row. The student loan people haven't garnished my wages . . . yet. I can tell a good joke. I can remember the names and ages of all my kids. I remembered to give my mother a card on Mother's Day last year. Or was that two years ago? Once I told a girlfriend that her new hairdo was nice even though it looked like her neck just threw up.

If I think hard enough, I can come up with many wonderful, positive qualities that I possess. If I think even harder, I might be able to come up with something I've accomplished since graduating, or at least outline a plan for something I'm going to do eventually that my mom can put in her Christmas newsletter.

Today I will give myself credit not only for what I have done, but for what I would like to do someday.

IDENTITY

I use heavy-gauge strings, tune low, play hard, and floor it.
Stevie Ray Vaughan

Did you ever see Stevie Ray Vaughan's guitar? What a beautiful piece of work. So well-worn there's hardly any finish left. Deep, sweat-stained grooves in the neck, nicks and burns from years of hard use.

Like me. I'm sweat-stained and deeply grooved also. I have nicks and burns from that time when I tried to use a soldering iron. Hell, I even have calluses from years of strenuous league bowling, and I can't even see my feet anymore when standing erect. Now that's hard use!

When I think of the life I've lived, and the scars I bear, the blues I've wished I could sing but can't because my voice is shot, too, I see that I am one beautiful instrument.

If I paint myself purple and attach some strings at my neck, maybe Susanna Hoffs will want to strum me.

COURAGE

I am the greatest.

Muhammad Ali

Face it: if you can say it, and mean it, then you can be it. Live any theory, even a wrong one, long enough and it becomes true. It worked for Ali. It works for the majority of monarchs and all politicians.

Go ahead, say it, just once. Say, Dammit, I am one hell of a guy. I am an all-around, happening kind of dude. I'm the big cheese, the bee's knees, the cat's pajamas. Despite what my ex-wife, my kids, and even my mother are saying about me lately, I am the crème de la crème, passing through life, imparting that ineffable je ne sais quois to everyone and everything around me. I am an apotheosis of myself. I am my own best friend, my comrade in arms. I am my own hero.

Honk if you love yourself.

SELF-ACCEPTANCE

It's not the meat, it's the motion.

Bulgarian proverb

I am just right! Sometimes I have suspected otherwise. Others have tried to tell me that I am too much. Like the time I tried to get my date to pay for dinner by declaring that I was a feminist and therefore felt that gender specifications with regard to dinner tabs was a slap in the face of liberated women everywhere. After she paid up (I left the tip—hey, I'm not a total slouch) I asked her in for a nightcap. That's when she told me I was too much. One time a date told me I was too little, but I don't like to talk about that.

What a relief to realize that I am just right, neither too much nor too little, but a healthy, respectable, undisputable, substantial, well-orchestrated, intensely mobile, neither understated nor overstated, neither diminutive nor pronounced, but a considerably well-rigged, well-maintained, and well-balanced five inches.

Today, I will sit and be just right. Then tomorrow, maybe I'll be just right with that girl in the French-cut bikini who sells foot-long hot dogs on the corner. I mean, how's she gonna tell the difference in the dark?

ALTERNATIVES/WORK

It's no credit to anyone to work too hard.

E. W. Howe

Contrary to popular belief, we Men Who Do Next to Nothing are constantly doing something. Just because we're not getting paid for it doesn't mean that we aren't making excellent use of each and every day.

There's the lost episodes of Spiderman to catch up on, the sock drawer to organize, and I could wax the Mustang, too, even though it doesn't run right now. Still, that car's a classic, and I've got to protect the finish, because I'm gonna sell that baby for some serious dollar someday, and then I'm gonna buy a guitar and start a rock and roll band and tour the world and make zillions of dollars and get laid every single night by beautiful babes in fish-net stockings who all have alter egos that are German and look really good in midnight blue leather.

Then I'll be really busy, but until then, I have plenty here to occupy my time. I could hang up a hammock in the other corner of the yard, in case Dad is using this one when I feel like lying down.

I wonder how much guitar lessons cost?

CREATIVITY

Every man of genius sees the world at a different angle from his fellows.

Havelock Ellis

I love the image of the back door. All men of vision approach the world from new directions. I, for instance, always make my approach through the back door. I love the thought of secret, out-of-the-way entrances. I love spending the afternoon contemplating what wonderful and surprising sensations await me on the other side of that unexplored gate.

I suppose the real idea is not the back door per se; it's the willingness to explore new paths, to go in through the out door.

I need more back doors in my life.

Getting in the back door may not be easy, but if they don't see you coming, they can't stop you at the gate or collect the price of admission.

INSPIRATION

Inspiration is never genuine.

Samuel Butler

Sometimes we forget that to do our work well, no matter what it is, we must be inspired. This is true for any kind of work, be it paid or otherwise, which explains why I haven't been able to do any for quite some time now. Inspiration is the piston in our cylinder, the spark in our plugs, and as I haven't had a tune-up in about eight months now, inspiration is just about entirely out of the question.

I don't know why my mother doesn't understand this. I try to explain this to her. And I also add that inspiration does not come on demand. Like any process, it is a mystery and does not answer when called, but comes, uninvited, and expects not only a beer, but a beer glass.

Inspiration is a real pain in the ass and somebody I'd never willingly sit down and have a beer with, 'cause you just can't depend on him. I mean, you give him a beer, you turn around to slap him on the back, where is he? He's disappeared, and you're sitting there, a dumb schmuck, with a dirty glass, and when you go to the fridge you realize the beer's all gone. I mean, what kind of a guest is that?

When I wait for inspiration, I always end up making another beer run.

INSTINCT/ANIMAL NATURE

Mglfwabogtrmslztsff.

Kurt Cobain

Any man who has sat in the park and watched a dog lift his leg on a tree, any man who has witnessed this unabashed and free-flowing expression of masculinity, knows the beauty of animal instinct.

How often do our own pure instincts become clouded with civility and politeness? How easy it is to lose sight of the men we truly are. What a far better world it would be if we allowed ourselves to express our essential selves.

Who we are is inextricably linked with what we are. We are men and like the spaniel must lift our legs often to mark our territory, to write our names proudly in the snow, and to claim every bitch on this side of the avenue as our property.

To be a man I have to pee.

PANIC/FATIGUE

Jane, stop this crazy thing!

George Jetson

Living our lives can be so exhausting. Writing down phone messages, parking only in designated areas, and leaving the toilet seat down can be monumental burdens. Sometimes it feels like life is one responsibility after another, leaving us drained and despondent, and, in return, granting us only an illusion of control.

We are caught on a treadmill, strapped to a rowing machine, chained to a Stairmaster, with no big-breasted, Spandex-clad aerobics instructor in sight. Could it be that we are creating our own inner turmoil, that conflicts and crises do not just happen to us, but are self-perpetuated? Wouldn't it be better to admit that we are totally out of control?

Isn't it preferable to leave your shoes untied, your zipper unzipped, or better yet, just not to get dressed at all? Might not the elimination of all activity from our lives grant us the serenity we seek?

I hope I will allow myself to see that an illusion of control is not worth the effort.

ROMANCE

Love'll get you like a case of Bovine Encephalitis.
Croatian shepherd's saying

Sometimes, when I'm feeling particularly lonely and unlovable, my mother takes the opportunity to tell me that there's a trick to attracting women. She says that if I put on a nice suit, shave, and get a haircut, or a job, this will make others love me. I don't think so.

I mean, she's my mother, what does she know about love? She probably hasn't had any in about two hundred years. My father went into a walking coma back around 1969, the year we lost the pennant race by one run, and he hasn't uttered a sound since. He can still do the important things, like operate the BarcaLounger and the remote control, but let's face it, his Don Juan days are over. She drove him to it, always insisting that he put on a suit, shave, and get a haircut or a job. She did it to him, and now she's doing it to me. It's just like her, too, to choose these moments when I'm feeling down to sink her hooks into me and try to get me to conform to her expectations.

Loving is letting go of expectations and letting people be who they are. If my mother really loved me, she'd get off it already and start baking me some of the miniwienies wrapped in the Poppin' Fresh rolls. Now that would be helpful and loving.

In a world with miniwienies, who needs love?

HOLIDAYS

Bah . . . humbug!

Charles Dickens

Christmas is coming, and already I feel exhausted and overwhelmed. It is so difficult to maintain my daily rituals and routines when she's in a frenzy of gift buying, decorating, baking, entertaining, and just generally running around being cloyingly annoying. All that stuff was okay when I was a kid, but why does she have to bother now? I'm not five years old anymore, and I'm beginning to suspect that I'm allergic to tinsel because every time I walk by that damn tree I get hives. Besides, I can't afford Christmas on an ex–barrel reamer's unemployment benefits, so why does she have to go and rub it in?

I have to face it. I am dreading the holiday season. Perhaps it is time for me to take stock and reevaluate whether or not it is truly important to me to have to go through this every year. Is all of the mind-bending activity around here really worth the vented boxer shorts and the eight-pack of tube socks that is always waiting for me under the tree?

Maybe I should check into the YMCA for a week. Wait, did I pay them yet for last Christmas?

BECOMING A MAN

The fox condemns the trap, not himself.

William Blake

In our shallow, materialistic society, so much emphasis is placed upon financial success that we have very few role models for manliness. Without any instruction manual, we are suddenly expected to be men and have the wage ceiling and bank balance of our fathers.

In a society that knows absolutely nothing about it (or if they do, they're certainly not telling us), there is the assumption that one is a little boy, and then suddenly one is a systems analyst. In our bourgeois, hedonistic, brutalizing culture, becoming a man is linked with making a lot of money. But manhood is much more than a pay stub or a bank balance. Manhood is about hanging out in bars drinking dollar drafts and talking about sports, and Rocky, and the Terminator, and the Dallas Cowboys cheerleaders. Manhood is vintage Mustangs, and pre-CBS Fender guitars, heavy metal, and fly girls. Manhood is telling my mother that I won't turn down the TV, shave, or go job hunting tomorrow because I don't need those external yardsticks to measure my value as a man.

I am just being a man, so get off my case.

WOMEN

Nowadays, we're more into staying in our rooms and reading Nietzsche.

Robert Plant

Sex has become very complicated, even for rock stars. I myself decided to stay away from professional women because I was sick and tired of feeling like a slave to success. I wanted to avoid that trap. Lately I've found that any woman can become a trap, whether she's a homemaker, aerobics instructor, toll collector, cocktail waitress, vice president of Finance or Purchasing, or my mother. They're all the same.

I need to recognize that all of them, regardless of what they do, are ultimately part of the "materialistic" world. Even when they start out on the bottom of the professional ladder, like as a purchasing clerk, next thing I know, she's getting promoted and demanding that I do the same.

And does she care if I was working for a fascist who didn't care if it took all night as long as I met my barrel quota? Does she care if I worked for an abusive tyrant who didn't care if I was sick or tired and who didn't think twice about insisting that I work overtime and miss the heavyweight championship fight on Pay-Per-View, even though I already paid for it? What was I supposed to do? I had to quit. My honor was at stake. But did she understand? No. And what's worse, my mother is on her side. She's always on her side.

This isn't a third world country, this is America, and oppression costs more than $4.35 an hour.

LAUGHTER

To laugh means to love mischief.

Friedrich Nietzsche

One of my better moments was when I was invited to give that presentation to the board of directors at my old company. I was a little anxious, so right before going on stage I went to the executive lounge to expel all of my anxieties. I came out feeling pretty cocky. And when I hit that stage, I made a real impression. Everybody's attention was on me. You could have heard a pin drop. That was the clearest and most articulate presentation I ever gave, and I could see in their eyes, as I gave my forecasts, that they were with me every step of the way. I had them in the palm of my hand.

Of course, halfway through my speech I realized that they weren't in my palm, but in my lap. I had forgotten to zip up my fly, and as it was a Tuesday, I wasn't wearing any underwear. I got a little uncomfortable for a minute, began to lose my cool, but then I remembered that at moments like these, laughter is a healing balm. So I cracked a joke. You know, that one about the pearl diver and the eel? Sure made a rousing closer for my speech.

When they see how funny we are, they see how precious we are.

COMPROMISE/CONVICTIONS

Two all beef patties, special sauce, lettuce, cheese, pickles, onions, on a sesame seed bun.

McDonald's slogan

The Big Mac. What a glorious monument to men and meat. I have a friend who prefers The Whopper. We don't see each other much anymore.

Some things a man just can't compromise on. I learned that from Bob. Bob was my pet chameleon, and he was a reptile who knew how to compromise. Whatever he was sitting on, he'd turn that same color. For instance, if he was sitting on a gray rock, he'd turn gray. Bob was flexible, but he had his limits. One time, I bought a fluorescent green bridge. You know, one of those glow-in-the-dark numbers you put in your fish tank, although when you think of it, why would a fish need a bridge, anyway? Anyway, I put Bob on the bridge, but no matter how many ants I fed him, he wouldn't turn chartreuse.

I learned a lot from Bob. He was a chameleon of character who stuck courageously to his own spectrum, and would only eat live ants and McDonald's beef. Bob has since died. Karl, my Gila monster, ate him, along with about two tablespoons of Burger King hamburger that Bob had refused just two hours before.

I learned three important lessons from Bob that will live with me forever. Never eat dead ants, never turn chartreuse, and never, ever, hang out with Gila monsters who prefer Burger King.